W9-DFC-740

THE
Rock Classics
BOOK

ISBN 0-7935-8312-8

HAL•LEONARD®
CORPORATION

7777 W. BLUEMOUND RD. P.O. BOX 13819 MILWAUKEE, WI 53213

Visit Hal Leonard Online at
www.halleonard.com

THE Rock Classics BOOK

CONTENTS

STRUM AND PICK PATTERNS

This chart contains the suggested strum and pick patterns that are referred to by number at the beginning
of each song in this book. The symbols ⊓ and ∨ in the strum patterns refer to down and up strokes, respectively.
The letters in the pick patterns indicate which right-hand fingers plays which strings.

p = thumb
i = index finger
m = middle finger
a = ring finger

For example; Pick Pattern 2
is played: thumb - index - middle - ring

Strum Patterns

Pick Patterns

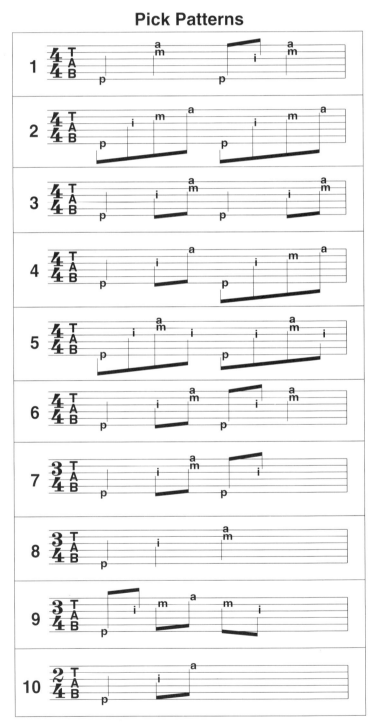

You can use the 3/4 Strum or Pick Patterns in songs written in compound meter (6/8, 9/8, 12/8, etc.).
For example, you can accompany a song in 6/8 by playing the 3/4 pattern twice in each measure.
The 4/4 Strum and Pick Patterns can be used for songs written in cut time (¢) by doubling the note
time values in the patterns. Each pattern would therefore last two measures in cut time.

All Day and All of the Night

Words and Music by Ray Davies

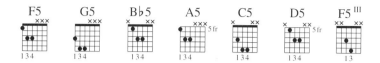

F5   G5   Bb5   A5   C5   D5   F5 III

Strum Pattern: 2
Pick Pattern: 6

Intro
Bright Rock

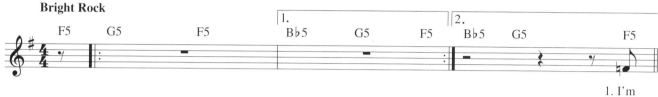

1. I'm

Verse

not con-tent to be with you __ in the day - time.

2. *See Additional Lyrics*

Girl, I want to be with you __ all of the time. The

Pre-Chorus   **Chorus**

on-ly time I feel all right __ is by your __ side. ____ Girl, I want to

be with you __ all of the __ time, all day and all of the night. __ All day and

all of the night. __ All day and all of the night. __

Additional Lyrics

2. I believe that you and me last forever.
Oh yeah, all day and night time, yours; leave me never.

Addicted to Love

Words and Music by Robert Palmer

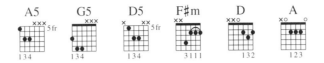

Strum Pattern: 6
Pick Pattern: 5

Verse

Moderate Rock

1. The lights are on but you're not home. Your mind ___ is not your
3. *See Additional Lyrics*
5. *Instrumental*

own. Your heart sweats, your bod-y shakes; an-oth-er kiss is what it

Verse

takes. 2. You can't sleep, you can't eat. There's no doubt ___ you're in
4., 6. *See Additional Lyrics*

deep. ___ Your throat is tight, you can't breathe; ___ an-oth-er

Bridge

kiss is all you need. Oh, ___ you ___ like to think that you're im-mune ___ to the stuff, oh yeah. ___

___ It's clos-er to the truth to say you can't get e-nough, you know you're

1.
gon-na have to face it; you're ad-dict-ed to love. 3. You see the
2.
gon-na have to face it; you're ad-

Chorus

dict-ed to love. ___ Might as well face it, you're ad-dict-ed to love. ___ Might

Additional Lyrics

3. You see the signs but you can't read.
   You're running at a dif'rent speed.
   Your heart beats in double time;
   Another kiss and you'll be mine.

4. A one track mind, you can't be saved.
   Oblivion is all you crave.
   If there's some left for you,
   You don't mind if you do.

6. The lights are on but you're not home.
   Your will is not your own.
   Your heart sweats, your teeth grind;
   Another kiss and you'll be mine.

Babe, I'm Gonna Leave You

Words and Music by Anne Bredon, Jimmy Page and Robert Plant

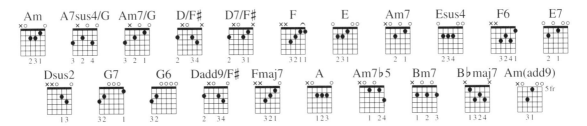

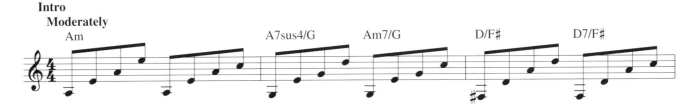

Strum Pattern: 4
Pick Pattern: 2

Intro
Moderately

1. Babe,
2. *See Additional Lyrics*

ba - by, ba - by,

I'm gon-na leave __ you.

I said ____ ba - by, ____

you know __ I'm gon - na leave ____ you. ____

I'll _____ leave you __ when the sum-mer time, __ leave you when the

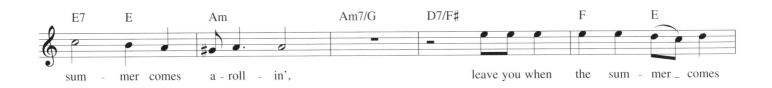

sum - mer comes a - roll - in', leave you when the sum - mer __ comes

go a - way. _____ Oh, ____ huh.

So good, sweet ba - by. __ It was real-ly,

real - ly good. _ You made me hap-py ev-'ry sin-gle day,

but now _ I've got to go a - way. _____ Oh,

oh, oh.

Ba - by, __ ba - by, __ ba - by, __

Freely

that's when it's call - in' me, __ I said that's when it's call - in' me, __

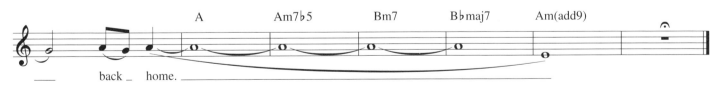

back _ home. __

Additional Lyrics

2. Babe, babe, babe, babe, babe, babe,
Baby, mm, baby I wanna leave you.
I ain't jokin' woman, I got to ramble.
Oh, yeah. Baby, baby, I will leave you,
I've really got to ramble.
I can hear it callin' me the way it used to do,
I can hear it callin' me back home.

Back in the Saddle

Words and Music by Steven Tyler and Joe Perry

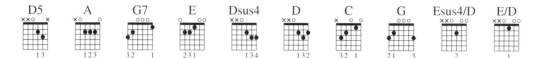

Strum Pattern: 3, 5
Pick Pattern: 3, 5

Intro
Moderate Hard Rock Beat

I'm back, I'm

back in the sad-dle a - gain. __ I'm back, I'm back in the sad-dle a -

gain. __ 1. Rid-in' in-to town a - lone by the light of the moon, __
2. *See Additional Lyrics*

I'm look-in' for old Su - kie Jones, __ she cra-zy horse sa - loon. ___

Bar Keep gim-me a drink, that's when she caught my eye. __ She

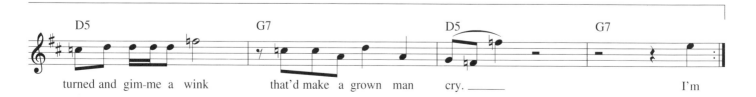

turned and gim-me a wink that'd make a grown man cry. ___ I'm

Additional Lyrics

2. Come easy, go easy alright till the risin' sun.
   I'm callin' all the shots tonight, I'm like a loaded gun.

Pre-Chorus I'm ridin', I'm shinin' up my saddle.
              I'm ridin', the snake is gonna rattle.

Bad Case of Loving You

Words and Music by John Moon Martin

Strum Pattern: 2
Pick Pattern: 4

Intro
Moderate Rock

1. Hot sum-mer night ___ fell like a net; ___ I got-ta
2., 3. *See Additional Lyrics*

find ___ my ba-by yet. ___ I need you, to soothe my

head, to turn my blue heart to red. ___

Chorus

Doc-tor, doc-tor, give me the news, ___ I got-ta bad case of lov-in' you. ___

To Coda

No pill's gon-na cure my ill, ___ I got-ta bad case of lov - in' you. ___

2. A pret-ty face ___

Bridge

I know you like ___ it, you like it on top.

Tell me ma - ma, are you gon - na stop? _____

3. You had me down, _

Additional Lyrics

2. A pretty face don't make no pretty heart.
   I learned that buddy from the start.
   You think I'm cute, a little bit shy,
   Mama, I ain't that kind of guy.

3. You had me down, twenty to zip.
   A smile of Judas on your lip.
   Shake my fist, knock on wood.
   I got it bad and I got it good.

Ballroom Blitz

Words and Music by Mike Chapman and Nicky Chinn

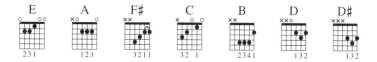

Strum Pattern: 1
Pick Pattern: 2

Intro
Moderate Rock

Spoken: Are you ready, Steve? Uh, huh.   *Andy?*   *Yeah!*   *Mick?*

O.K.   *All right, fellas.*   *Let's go!*

Additional Lyrics

2. I'm reaching out for something.
   Touching nothing's all I ever do.
   Oh, I softly call you over,
   When you appear there's nothing left of you. Uh, huh.
   Now the man at the back is ready to crack
   As he raises his hands to the sky.
   And the girl in the corner is ev'ryone's mourner,
   She could kill you with a wink of her eye.

Pre-Chorus 2. Oh yeah, it was electric, so frightfully hectic
   And the band started leaping, cause they all stopped breathing.
   Yeah, yeah, yeah, yeah, yeah.

Badge

Words and Music by Eric Clapton and George Harrison

Strum Pattern: 4
Pick Pattern: 6

Intro
Moderately

%Verse

1. Think-in' 'bout the times you drove _ in my car.
2., 3. *See Additional Lyrics*

Think-in' that I might have drove _ you too far.

And I'm think-in' 'bout the love that you laid on my ta -

To Coda

- ble.

Yes, I told

Chorus

you that the light goes up and down. _ Don't you no - tice how the wheel goes

round. And you bet - ter pick your-self up from the ground _ be - fore _ they bring the cur - tain down. _

D.S. al Coda

Coda

_ Yes, be - fore _ they bring the cur - tain down. _

Additional Lyrics

2. I told you not to wander 'round in the dark.
I told you 'bout the swans, that they live in the park.
Then I told you 'bout our kid, now he's married to Mabel.

3. Talkin' 'bout a girl that looks quite like you.
She didn't have the time to wait in the queue.
She cried away her life since she fell off the cradle.

Bang a Gong (Get It On)

Words and Music by Marc Bolan

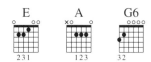

Strum Pattern: 3
Pick Pattern: 3

⊕ *Coda*

Outro-Chorus *Repeat and Fade*

Get it on, _____ bang a gong. _ Get it on. _____ Get it on, _

Additional Lyrics

2. Well, you're built like a car;
   You've got a hub cap diamond star halo.
   You're built like a car, oh yeah.
   Well, you're an untamed youth,
   That's the truth, with your cloak full of eagles.
   You're dirty, sweet and you're my girl.

3. Well, you're windy and wild.
   You've got the blues in your shoes and your stockings.
   You're windy and wild, oh yeah.
   Well, you're built like a car;
   You've got a hub cap diamond star halo.
   You're dirty, sweet and you're my girl.

4. Well, you're dirty and sweet,
   Clad in black, don't look back and I love you.
   You're dirty and sweet, oh yeah.
   Well, you dance when you walk.
   So let's dance, take a chance, understand me.
   You're dirty, sweet and you're my girl.

Bennie and the Jets

Words and Music by Elton John and Bernie Taupin

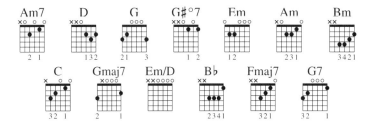

Strum Pattern: 2
Pick Pattern: 3

Verse
Moderately Slow

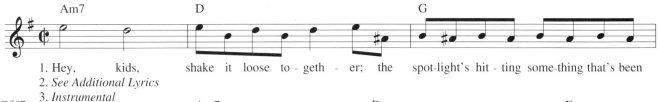

1. Hey, kids, shake it loose to - geth - er; the spot-light's hit - ting some-thing that's been
2. *See Additional Lyrics*
3. *Instrumental*

known to change the weath-er. We'll kill the fat - ted calf to - night, so stick a - round.

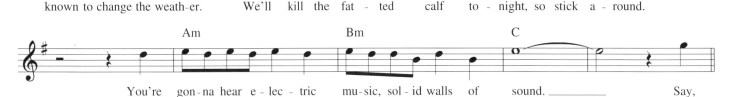

You're gon-na hear e - lec - tric mu-sic, sol - id walls of sound. _____ Say,

Bell Bottom Blues

Words and Music by Eric Clapton

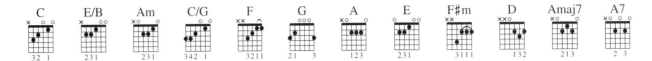

C   E/B   Am   C/G   F   G   A   E   F#m   D   Amaj7   A7

Strum Pattern: 4
Pick Pattern: 4

Slow Rock

Verse

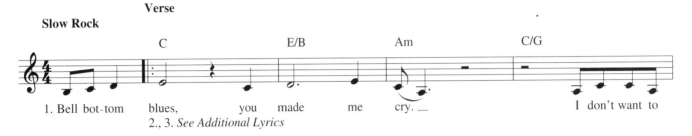

C   E/B   Am   C/G

1. Bell bot-tom blues, you made me cry. __ I don't want to
2., 3. *See Additional Lyrics*

F   G   F   C   G   C

lose __ this feel - in'.   If I could choose __

E/B   Am   C/G   F   G

a place __ to die, __   it would be in ___ your __ arms.

Chorus

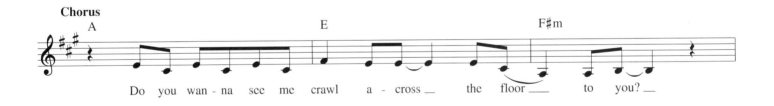

A   E   F#m

Do you wan-na see me crawl a - cross __ the floor ___ to you? __

D   E   A   E

Do you wan-na hear me beg you to take me back?

F#m   D   E   A

__ I'd glad - ly do it be - cause I don't want to

fade a - way. _____ Give me one ___ more day, ___

___ please. I don't want to fade a - way. _____

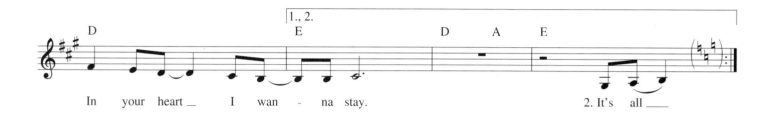

In your heart ___ I wan - na stay. 2. It's all ___

3.

Outro

- na stay. I don't want to fade a - way. _____

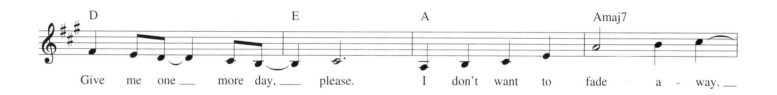

Give me one ___ more day, ___ please. I don't want to fade a - way. ___

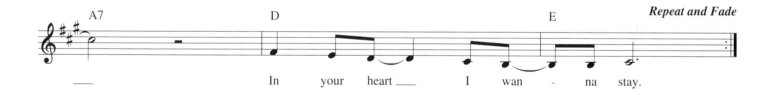

Repeat and Fade

In your heart ___ I wan - na stay.

Additional Lyrics

2. It's all wrong, but it's all right,
   The way that you treat me, baby.
   Once I was strong, but I lost the fight.
   You won't find a better loser.

3. Bell bottom blues, don't say goodbye.
   I'm sure we're gonna meet again.
   And if we do, don't ya be surprised
   If you find me with another lover.

The Best of My Love

Words and Music by John David Souther, Don Henley and Glenn Frey

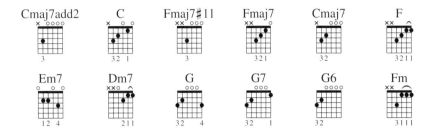

Strum Pattern: 1, 2
Pick Pattern: 1, 2

Intro

Moderately Slow

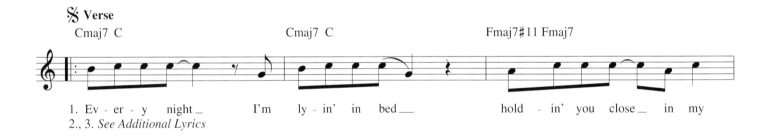

1. Ev - er - y night __ I'm ly - in' in bed __ hold - in' you close __ in my
2., 3. *See Additional Lyrics*

dreams; __ think - in' a - bout __ all the things that we __ said and

com - in' a - part __ at the seams. __ We tried to talk it o -

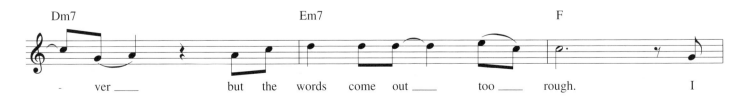

- ver __ but the words come out __ too __ rough. I

know you were try - in' to give me the best __ of your __ love.

1.   **2.**   **Chorus**

(Whoa, _____ sweet dar -

You get the best of my __ love, you get the best of my __ love. __

- lin'.)   (Whoa _____

__ sweet dar - lin'.)   You get the best of my love, __ you get the best of my __

Bridge

love. _____   Oo, __ I'm go - in' back in time __ an' it's a

sweet _____ dream.   It was a qui - et night __ and I would

D.S. al Coda

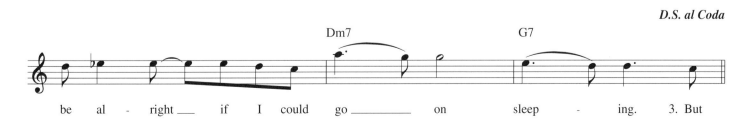

be al - right __ if I could go _____ on sleep - ing.   3. But

⊕ *Coda*

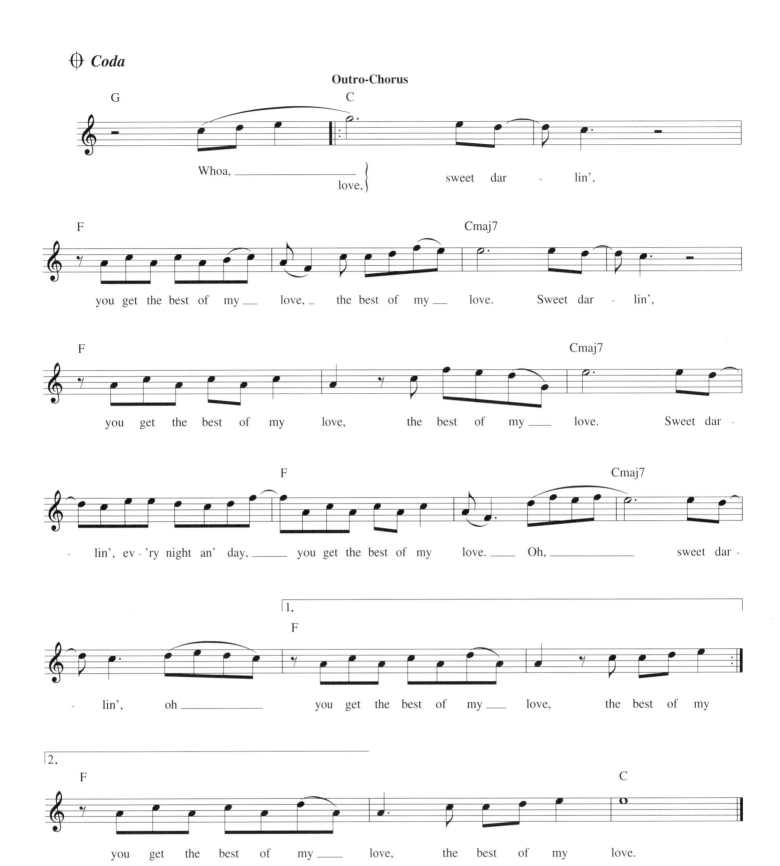

Additional Lyrics

2. Beautiful faces an' loud empty places, look at the way we live;
   Wastin' our time on cheap talk and wine, left us so little to give.
   That same old crowd was like a cold dark cloud that we could never rise above.
   But here in my heart I give you the best of my love.

3. But ev'ry morning I wake up and worry what's gonna happen today.
   You see it your way and I see it mine but we both see it slippin' away.
   You know we always had each other, baby, I guess that wasn't enough;
   Oh, oh, but here in my heart I give you the best of my love.

Day Tripper

Words and Music by John Lennon and Paul McCartney

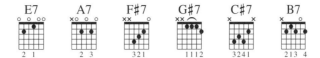

Strum Pattern: 2, 5
Pick Pattern: 4

Intro
Moderate Rock

1. Got a good rea-son for tak-ing the eas-y way out. ___
2., 3. *See Additional Lyrics*

Got a good rea-son for tak-ing the eas-y way out, ___ now. She was a

day _____ trip-per, { 1., 2. one way tick-et, } yeah. It took me
{ 3. Sun-day driv-er, }

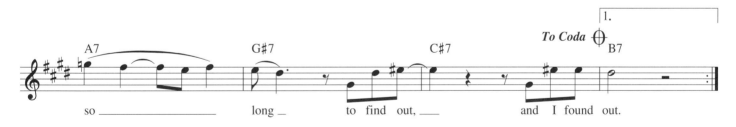

so _____ long ___ to find out, ___ and I found out.

out.

⊕ **Coda**

Outro

play 4 times

B7   E7

out.

Repeat and Fade

Day trip-per,   day trip-per,   yeah.

Additional Lyrics

2. She's a big teaser.
   She took me half the way there.
   She's a big teaser.
   She took me half the way there, now.

3. Tried to please her.
   She only played one night stands.
   Tried to please her.
   She only played one night stands, now.

Detroit Rock City

Words and Music by Paul Stanley and Bob Ezrin

A5   C5   D5   G5   F5

Strum Pattern: 1
Pick Pattern: 1

Intro
Fast Rock

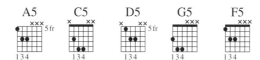

A5

C5   D5

1. I

Verse

A5

feel   up-tight   on a   Sat-ur-day   night.   Nine   o-clock,   the

2., 3., 4. See Additional Lyrics

ra - di - o's the on - ly light.   I   hear   my   song   and   it   pulls   me   through.

Comes on strong;   tells me what I   got   to   do.   I   got   to   get

Chorus

up! Ev - 'ry - bod - y's gon - na move their feet. Get down! Ev - 'ry - bod - y's gon - na

leave   their   seat.   You   got - ta lose your mind   in   De - troit   Rock

Cit - y.   Get   up! Ev - 'ry - bod - y's gon - na move their feet. Get

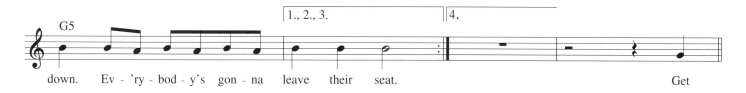

down. Ev - 'ry - bod - y's gon - na leave their seat.   Get

Outro

up! Ev - 'ry - bod - y's gon - na leave their seat. Get down!

Additional Lyrics

2. Gettin' late, I just can't wait.
   Ten o'clock, and I know I gotta hit the road.
   First I drink, then I smoke.
   Start up the car and I try to make the midnight show.

3. Movin' fast doin' ninety five.
   Hit top speed, but I'm still movin' much too slow.
   Feel so good; I'm so alive.
   Hear my song, playin' on the radio. It goes;

4. Twelve o'clock, I gotta rock.
   There's a truck ahead, lights starin' at my eyes.
   Whoa, my God, no time to turn,
   I got to laugh, 'cause I know I'm gonna die. Why?

Brass in Pocket

Words and Music by Chrissie Hynde and James Honeyman-Scott

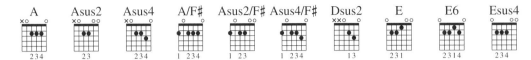

Strum Pattern: 1, 3
Pick Pattern: 1, 2

Intro
Moderate Rock

1. Got brass _

in pock-et,   got bot-tle   I'm _ gon-na use _ it.   In - ten-tion,

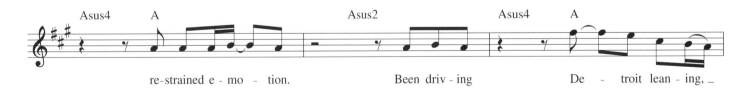

I feel in-ven-tive, __   gon-na make you, make you, make you no - tice. _____   2. Got mo-tion,
3. *See Additional Lyrics*

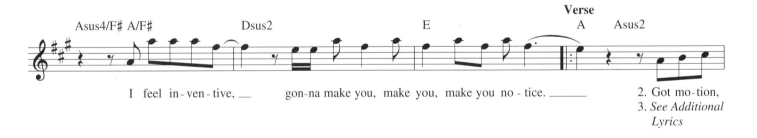

re-strained e - mo - tion.   Been driv-ing   De - troit lean-ing, _

no rea - son _____   it seems so pleas - ing. _____   Gon-na make you,   make

Additional Lyrics

3. Got rhythm, I can't miss a beat.
   I got new skank so reet,
   Got something I'm winking at you.
   Gonna make you, make you, make you notice.

Brown Eyed Girl

Words and Music by Van Morrison

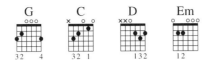

Strum Pattern: 6
Pick Pattern: 3

Intro
Moderately

1. Hey where did we ___ go? Days ___ when the rains ___ came,
2., 3. *See Additional Lyrics*

down ___ in the hol-low play-in' a new ___ game,

laugh-ing and a - run-ning, hey, ___ hey, skip-ping and a - jump-ing.

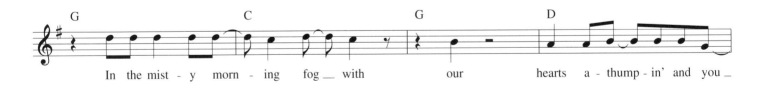

In the mist - y morn - ing fog ___ with our hearts a - thump-in' and you ___

___ my brown eyed girl. ___ You, ___ my ___

brown eyed girl. ___ Do you re - mem - ber when we used to sing; ___

Chorus

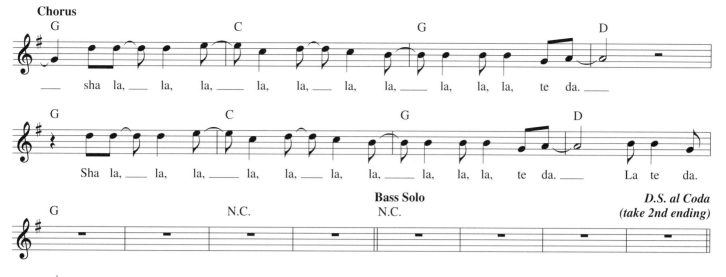

sha la, ___ la, ___ la, ___ la, ___ la, ___ la, la, ___ la, la, la, te da. ___

Sha la, ___ la, ___ la, ___ la, ___ la, ___ la, la, ___ la, la, la, te da. ___ La te da.

Bass Solo

D.S. al Coda
(take 2nd ending)

🜂 *Coda*

Outro-Chorus

Repeat and Fade

sha la, ___ la, ___ la, ___ la, ___ la, ___ la, ___ la, la, la, te da. ___

Additional Lyrics

2. Whatever happened to Tuesday and so slow,
   Going down the old mine with a transistor radio?
   Standing in the sunlight laughing,
   Hiding behind a rainbow's wall,
   Slipping and a-sliding
   All along the waterfall
   With you, my brown eyed girl.
   You, my brown eyed girl.
   Do you remember when we used to sing;

3. So hard to find my way, now that I'm all on my own.
   I saw you just the other day, my, how you have grown.
   Cast my memory back there, Lord,
   Sometimes I'm overcome thinking 'bout it.
   Making love in the green grass
   Behind the stadium
   With you, my brown eyed girl.
   You, my brown eyed girl.
   Do you remember when we used to sing;

Burning for You

Words and Music by Donald Roeser and Richard Meltzer

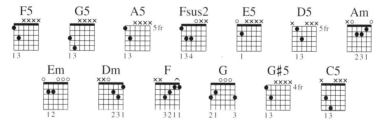

Strum Pattern: 3, 4
Pick Pattern: 3, 4

Intro
Moderately

Ahh. ___

Ahh. ___

⊕ **Coda**

Additional Lyrics

2. Time is the essence, time is the season.
Time ain't no reason, got no time to slow.
Time everlasting, time to play, "B - sides."
Time ain't on my side, time I'll never know.

Chorus Burn out the day, burn out the night.
I'm not the one to tell you what's wrong or what's right.
I've seen suns that were freezing and lives that were through.
But I'm burnin', I'm burnin', I'm burnin' for you.
I'm burnin', I'm burnin', I'm burnin' for you.

Caught Up in You

Words and Music by Frank Sullivan, Jim Peterik, Jeff Carlisi and Don Barnes

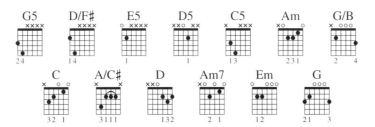

Strum Pattern: 3, 5
Pick Pattern: 3, 5

Verse
Moderately

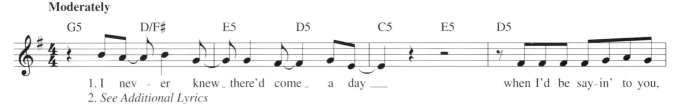

1. I nev - er knew there'd come a day ___ when I'd be say-in' to you,
2. *See Additional Lyrics*

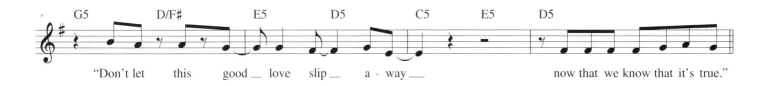

"Don't let this good ___ love slip ___ a - way ___ now that we know that it's true."

Pre-Chorus

Don't, don't you know ___ the kind of man I ___ am? ___ No, said I'd nev -
See Additional Lyrics

- er fall in love a - gain. But it's real, and the feel - ing comes ___ shin - ing through. ___

Chorus

___ I'm so caught up in you, ___ lit - tle girl, ___ { and I nev - } { you're the one ___ }

- er did sus - pect a ___ thing. } { ___ that's got me down on my knees. } So caught up in you, ___ lit - tle girl, ___ that I nev-

er want to get my-self free. And ba-by, it's true. ___ You're the one ___ who caught ___

___ me, ba - by, you taught ___ me how good it could be. ___ Fill your days ___

Bridge

___ and your nights, ___ no need to ev - er ask ___ me twice. ___ Oh no,

when-ev-er you want ___ me. And if ev - er comes a day ___ when you should

turn and walk ___ a - way, ___ oh no, I can't live with-out ___ you. ___

Interlude

I'm so caught up in you.

And if ev -

Bridge

er comes a day ___ when you should turn and walk ___ a - way, ___ oh

no, I can't live with - out ___ you. ___ I'm so caught up in you ___

Outro-Chorus

_lit - tle girl, ___ you're the one ___ that's got me down on my knees. So caught up in you, ___

_lit - tle girl, _____ that I nev - er want to get my-self free. And ba - by, it's true, ___

Repeat and Fade

_____ you're the one _____ who caught _ me, ba - by, you taught _ me how good it could be. ___

Additional Lyrics

2. It took so long to change my mind.
   I thought that love was a game.
   I played around enough to find
   No two are ever the same.

Pre-Chorus You made me realize the love I'd missed.
   So hot, love I couldn't quite resist.
   When it's right the light just comes shining through.

Crocodile Rock

Words and Music by Elton John and Bernie Taupin

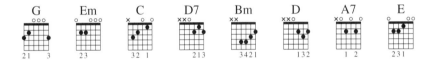

Strum Pattern: 2
Pick Pattern: 2

Verse
Fast Rock

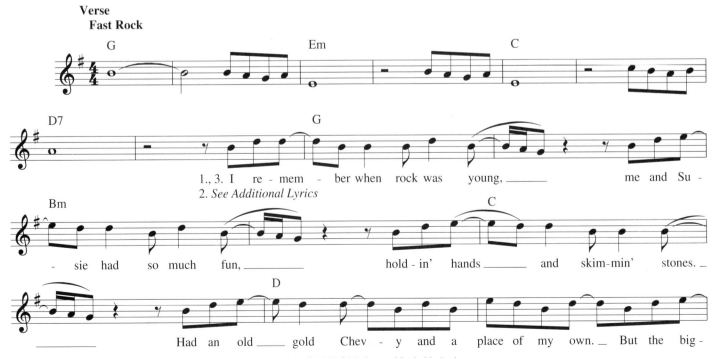

1., 3. I re - mem - ber when rock was young, ___ me and Su -

2. See Additional Lyrics

- sie had so much fun, _____ hold - in' hands _____ and skim-min' stones. ___

_____ Had an old ___ gold Chev - y and a place of my own. ___ But the big-

Additional Lyrics

2. But the years went by and rock just died.
   Susie went and left us for some foreign guy.
   Long nights cryin' by the record machine,
   Dreamin' of my Chevy and my old blue jeans.
   But they'll never kill the thrills we got
   Burnin' up to the Crocodile Rock.
   Learning fast as the weeks went past,
   We really thought the Crocodile Rock would last.

Centerfold

Words and Music by Seth Justman

Strum Pattern: 4
Pick Pattern: 6

Intro
Moderate Funk

play 4 times

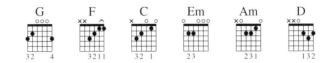

Na, na, na, na, na, na, na, na, na, na, na, na, na, na, na, na.

Verse

1. Does she walk? __ Does she talk? __ Does she come com - plete? My
2., 3. *See Additional Lyrics*

home - room, home - room an - gel al - ways pulled me from my seat.

She was pure like snow - flakes no one could ev - er stain; __ the

mem - o - ry of my an - gel could nev - er cause __ me pain. The

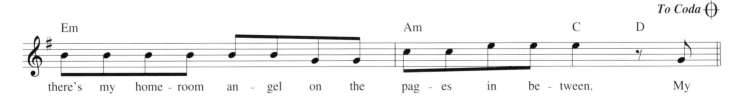

years go by; I'm look - in' through __ a gir - ly mag - a - zine; and

To Coda ⊕

there's my home - room an - gel on the pag - es in be - tween. My

Chorus

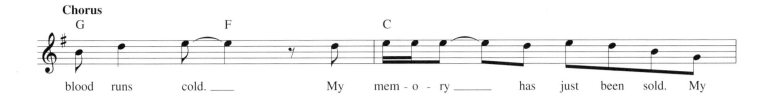

blood runs cold. ___ My mem - o - ry _____ has just been sold. My

an - gel is the cen-ter-fold, an - gel is the cen-ter-fold. My blood runs cold. _ My

2nd time, D.C. al Coda
(take repeat)

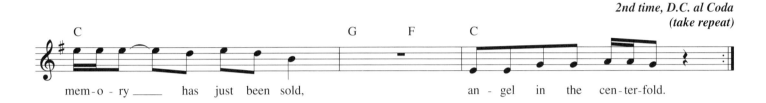

mem-o - ry _____ has just been sold, an - gel in the cen-ter-fold.

Coda

Na, na, na, na, na, na, na, na, na, na, na, na, na, na, na, na. _____ My

Outro-Chorus

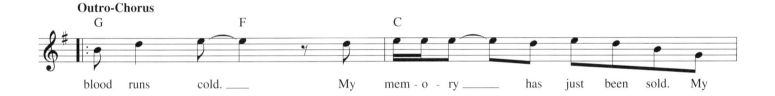

blood runs cold. ___ My mem - o - ry _____ has just been sold. My

Repeat and Fade

an - gel is the cen - ter - fold, an - gel is the cen - ter - fold. My

Additional Lyrics

2. Slipped me notes under the desk
   While I was thinkin' about her dress.
   I was shy, I turned away before she caught my eye.
   I was shakin' in my shoes
   Whenever she flashed those baby blues.
   Something had a hold on me when angel passed close by.
   Those soft, fuzzy sweaters, too magical to touch;
   To see her in that negligee is really just too much.

3. It's okay, I understand this ain't no never-never land.
   I hope that when this issue's gone,
   I'll see you when your clothes are on.
   Take your car, yes, we will. We'll take your car and drive it.
   Take it to a motel room and take 'em off in private.
   A part of me has just been ripped.
   The pages from my mind are stripped.
   Ah, no! I can't deny it. Oh yeah! I guess I gotta buy it.

Don't Fear The Reaper

Words and Music by Donald Roeser

Strum Pattern: 3
Pick Pattern: 2

Coda

(She had be-come like they __ are.) Come on, ba — by. (Don't fear the reap - er.)

Outro

Repeat and Fade

Additional Lyrics

3. Love of two is one.
   Here, but now they're gone.
   Come the last night of sadness,
   And it was clear that she couldn't go on. (Romeo and Juliet.)
   Then the door was open, and the wind appeared. (Like Romeo and Juliet.)
   The candles blew and then disappeared. (Redefine happiness.)
   The curtains flew, and then he appeared. (Saying, don't be afraid.)

Chorus Come on, baby. (And she had no fear.)
   And she ran to him. (Then they started to fly.)
   They looked backward and said goodbye. (She had become like they are.)
   She had taken his hand. (She had become like they are.)
   Come on, baby. (Don't fear the reaper.)

Evil Ways

Words and Music by Sonny Henry

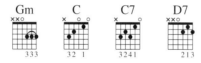

Strum Pattern: 6
Pick Pattern: 5

Verse

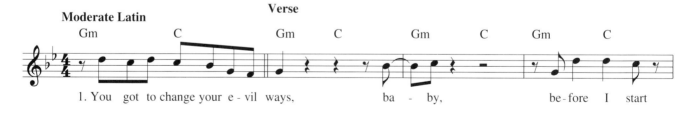

1. You got to change your e - vil ways, ba — by, be-fore I start

lov-in' you. You got to change, _ ba — by, and ev-'ry word _ that I

Drive My Car

Words and Music by John Lennon and Paul McCartney

Strum Pattern: 3
Pick Pattern: 4

Verse
Moderately

1. Asked a girl what she want-ed to be, ___ she said, "Ba-by, can't you see? ___

2., 3. *See Additional Lyrics*

I wan-na be fa-mous, a star of the screen, ___ but you can do some-thing in be - tween.

Chorus

Ba - by you can drive my car. ___ Yes, I'm gon-na be a star. ___

To Coda

Ba-by, you can drive my car, ___ and may-be I'll love ___ you." ___ you."

Beep, beep, mm, beep, beep, yeah! ___ "Ba-by, you can drive my car. ___

Yes, I'm gon-na be a star. ___ Ba-by, you can drive my car, ___ and may-be I'll love ___

D.C. al Coda

Coda

Outro

Repeat and Fade

___ you." ___ you." Beep, beep, mm, beep, beep, yeah! ___

Additional Lyrics

2. I told that girl that my prospects were good.
   She said, "Baby, it's understood,
   Working for peanuts is all very fine,
   But I can show you a better time.

3. I told that girl I could start right away,
   She said, "Baby, I've got something to say.
   I got no car and it's breakin' my heart,
   But I've found a driver, that's a start.

Free Ride

By Dan Hartman

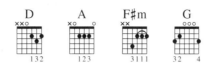

Strum Pattern: 6
Pick Pattern: 3

Verse
Moderate Rock

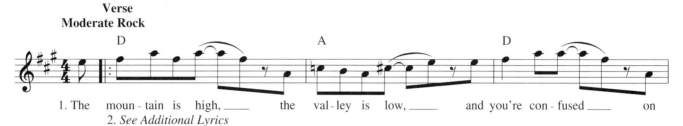

1. The moun-tain is high, _____ the val-ley is low, _____ and you're con-fused _____ on
2. *See Additional Lyrics*

which way to go. _____ So, I've come here _____ to give you a hand _____ and

lead you in - to the prom-ised land. _____ So, come on _____ and take a

free ride. _____ (Free ride. _____) Come on _____ and sit here by my side. _____

Come on _____ and take a free ride. 2. All

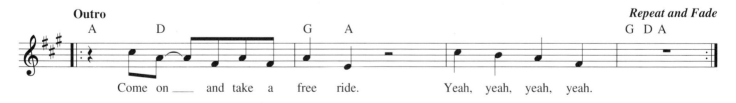

Come on _____ and take a free ride. Yeah, yeah, yeah, yeah.

Additional Lyrics

2. All over the country, I've seen it the same.
   Nobody's winning at this kind of game.
   We've gotta do better, it's time to begin.
   You know all the answers must come from within.

Eight Miles High

Words and Music by Roger McGuinn, David Crosby and Gene Clark

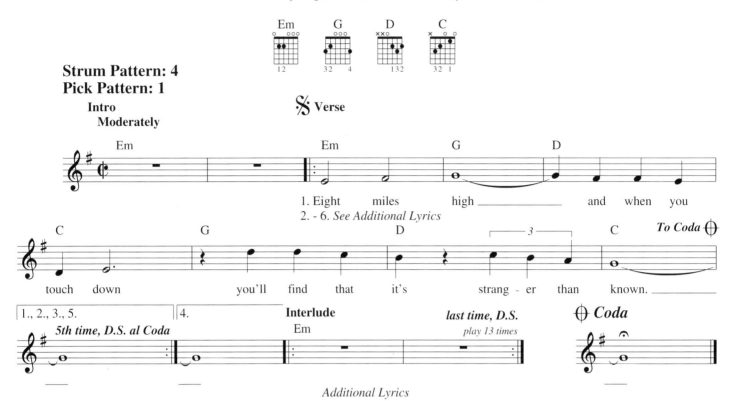

Strum Pattern: 4
Pick Pattern: 1

Intro
Moderately

1. Eight miles high _____ and when you
2. - 6. *See Additional Lyrics*

touch down you'll find that it's strang-er than known. _____

To Coda

5th time, D.S. al Coda

Interlude

last time, D.S.
play 13 times

Coda

Additional Lyrics

2. Signs in the street that say where you're going
   Are somewhere just being their own.

3. Nowhere is there warmth to be found
   Among those afraid of losing their ground.

4. Rain grey town, known for its sound.
   In places, small faces unbound.

5. 'Round the squares, huddled in storms.
   Some laughing, some just shapeless forms.

6. Sidewalk scenes and black limousines,
   Some living, some standing alone.

Eye of the Tiger

Theme from ROCKY III

Words and Music by Frank Sullivan and Jim Peterik

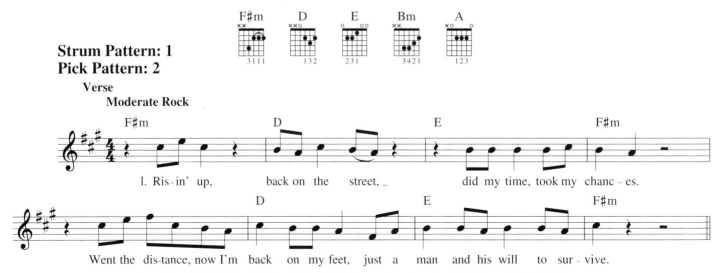

Strum Pattern: 1
Pick Pattern: 2

Verse
Moderate Rock

1. Ris-in' up, back on the street, ___ did my time, took my chanc - es.

Went the dis-tance, now I'm back on my feet, just a man and his will to sur - vive.

2. So man-y times it hap-pens too fast. ___ You trade your pas-sion for glo - ry.
3., 4. *See Additional Lyrics*

Don't lose your grip ___ on the dreams of the past, you must fight just to keep them a - live. It's the

eye of the ti - ger, it's the thrill of the fight, ___ ris - in' up to the chal-lenge of our

ri - val. And the last known sur - vi - vor stalks his prey in the night, and he's

watch - in' us all with the eye of the ti - ger. eye _____

_____ of the ti - ger.

The eye of the ti - ger. The eye of the

Additional Lyrics

3. Face to face, out in the heat,
   Hangin' tough, stayin' hungry.
   They stack the odds,
   Still we take to the street
   For the kill with the skill to survive.

4. Risin' up, straight to the top,
   Had the guts, got the glory.
   Went the distance,
   Now I'm not gonna stop,
   Just a man and his will to survive.

Emotional Rescue

Words and Music by Mick Jagger and Keith Richards

Strum Pattern: 3
Pick Pattern: 3

Verse
Moderately

1. Is there noth-ing I can say, noth-ing I can do to change your mind? I'm

so in love with you. You're too deep in, you can't get out. You're just a poor girl in a

rich man's house. __ Oo, oo, oo, oo, oo, oo, oo, oo. __ Oo, oo, oo, oo, oo,

oo, oo, oo. __ Yeah, ba-by, I'm cry-ing o-ver you.

Verse

2. Don't you know prom-is-es were nev-er meant to keep? Just like the night, they dis-
3., 4. *See Additional Lyrics*

Chorus

solve up in sleep. I'll be your sav-ior, stead-fast and true. I'll come to your e-mo-tion-al res-cue.

- tion-al res-cue. Oo, oo, oo, oo, oo, oo, oo, oo. __ Oo, oo, oo, oo, oo,

Additional Lyrics

3. You think you're one of a special breed.
   You think that you're his pet Pekinese.

Bridge I was dreaming last night,
   Last night I was dreaming,
   How you'd be mine.
   But I was crying, like a child,
   Yeah, I was crying, crying like a child.
   You will be mine, mine, mine, mine, mine, all mine.
   You could be mine, could be mine, mine all mine.

4. I come to you so silent in the night,
   So stealthy, so animal quiet.

Every Breath You Take

Written and Composed by Sting

Strum Pattern: 4
Pick Pattern: 3

Intro
Moderate Rock

Verse

1. Ev - 'ry breath you ___ take, ev - 'ry move you ___ make,
2. *See Additional Lyrics*

ev - 'ry bond ___ you break, ev - 'ry step ___ you take, I'll be watch-ing you. ___

2. Ev - 'ry sin - gle ___ I'll be watch-ing you. ___ Oh, can't you ___

Chorus

see you be-long to me. How my poor heart ___ aches ___

with ev - 'ry step ___ you take.   **Verse**   3., 4. Ev-'ry move you ___ make, ev - 'ry vow you ___

Additional Lyrics

2. Ev'ry single day, ev'ry word you say,
   Ev'ry game you play, ev'ry night you stay,
   I'll be watching you.

For Your Love

Words and Music by Graham Gouldman

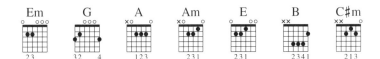

Strum Pattern: 4
Pick Pattern: 3

Intro
Bright Rock

For your love. ___

For your love. ___

Verse

1. I'd give you ev - 'ry - thing ___ and more and that's for sure. ___
2. *See Additional Lyrics*

For your love. ___ I'd bring you dia - mond rings ___ and

things right to your door. ___ For your love. ___ To thrill you with ___

Pre-Chorus

___ de - light, ___ I'd give you dia - monds bright. ___

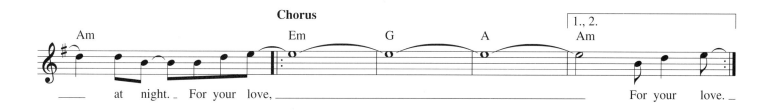

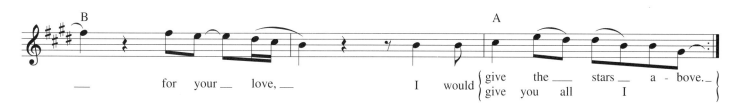

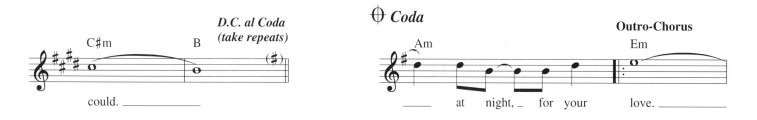

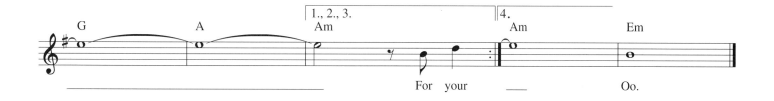

Additional Lyrics

2. I'd give the moon if it were mine to give.
For your love.
I'd give the stars and the sun 'fore I live.

55

Get Back

Words and Music by John Lennon and Paul McCartney

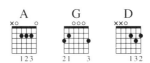

Strum Pattern: 1
Pick Pattern: 2

1. Jo - jo was a man who thought _ he was a lon - er, but _
2. *See Additional Lyrics*
3. *Instrumental*

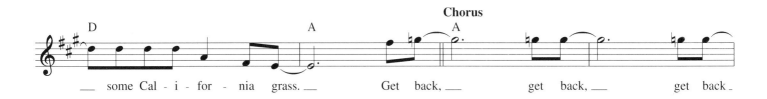

_ he knew it could-n't last. _ Jo - jo left his home in Tuc - son, Ar - i - zo - na, for

_ some Cal - i - for - nia grass. _ Get back, _ get back, _ get back _

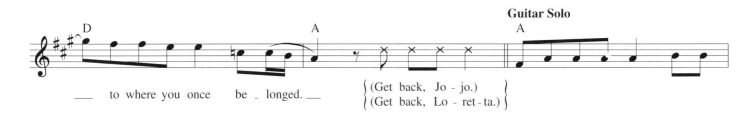

_ to where you once be - longed. _ Get back, _ get back, _ get back _

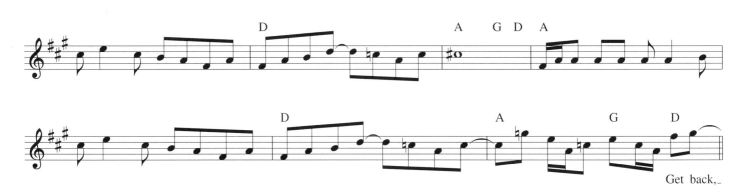

_ to where you once be _ longed. _

(Get back, Jo - jo.)
(Get back, Lo - ret - ta.)

Get back, _

Chorus

get back, ___ get back ___ to where you once be - longed. ___

Get back, ___ get back, ___ get back ___ to where you once be - longed. ___

1.

2.

D.S. and Fade

___ to where you once be - longed. ___

Additional Lyrics

2. Sweet Loretta Morgan thought she was a woman,
But she was another man.
All the girls around her say she's got it comin',
But she gets it while she can.

Gimme Some Lovin'

Words and Music by Spencer Davis, Muff Winwood and Steve Winwood

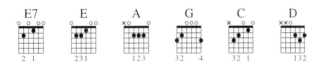

Strum Pattern: 1, 4
Pick Pattern: 3, 5

Intro
Moderately

Hey!

Verse

1. Well, my tem-p'ra-ture's ris - ing and my feet on the floor.
2., 3. *See Additional Lyrics*

Twen-ty peo-ple knock-in' 'cause they're want-ing some more. Let me in, ba-by. I don't

know what you've got. But you'd bet-ter take it eas-y. This ___ place is hot.

Pre-Chorus

To Coda

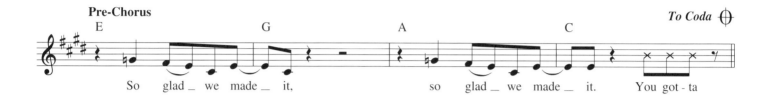

So glad ___ we made ___ it, so glad ___ we made ___ it. You got-ta

Chorus

gim-me some lov-in'. Gim-me some lov-in'. Gim-me some

lov - in' ev-er - y day.

D.S. al Coda

Hey! 2. Well, I 3. Well, I

Coda **Outro-Chorus**

Repeat and Fade

Gim-me some lov - in'. Gim-me some lov - in'.

Additional Lyrics

2. Well, I feel so good; ev'rything is sounding hot.
   Better take it easy, 'cause the place is on fire.
   Been a hard day and I don't know what to do.
   Wait a minute, baby. It could happen to you.

3. Well, I feel so good; ev'rybody's gettin' high.
   Better take it easy, 'cause the place is on fire.
   Been a hard day, nothin' went too good.
   Now I'm gonna relax, honey. Ev'rybody should.

Heartache Tonight

Words and Music by John David Souther, Don Henley, Glenn Frey and Bob Seger

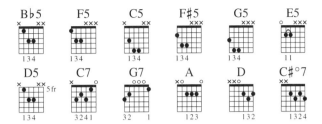

Strum Pattern: 3
Pick Pattern: 2, 3

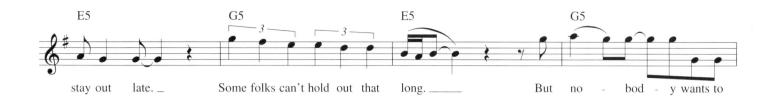

stay out late. ___ Some folks can't hold out that long. _____ But no - bod - y wants to

go home now; __ there's too much go - in' on. _____

This night is gon - na last for - ev - er. Last all, last all sum - mer

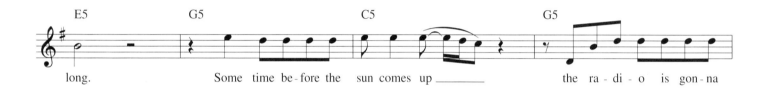

long. Some time be - fore the sun comes up _____ the ra - di - o is gon - na

Chorus

play that song. _____ There's gon - na be a heart - ache to - night, a

heart - ache to - night, I know. _____ There's gon - na be a

heart - ache to - night, a heart - ache to - night, I know. __ Lord, I

know. __ There's gon - na be a heart - ache to - night, the moon's shin - in' bright, so

turn out the light, and we'll get it right. __ There's gon-na be a heart - ache to - night, __ a

heart - ache to-night, I know. __

Coda

__ Let's go. _____ We can

Outro

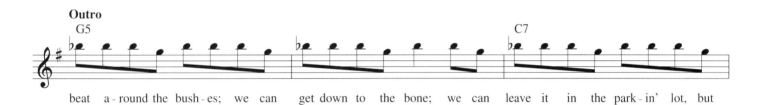

beat a - round the bush - es; we can get down to the bone; we can leave it in the park - in' lot, but

ei - ther way, there's gon - na be a heart-ache to - night, _____ a heart - ache to - night, I know. __

__ Oh, I know. __ There'll be a heart - ache to - night, _____ a

heart - ache to - night, I know. __

Green-Eyed Lady

Words and Music by Jerry Corbetta, J.C. Phillips and David Riordan

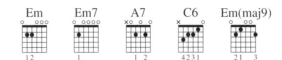

Strum Pattern: 4, 6
Pick Pattern: 4, 6

Intro
Moderate Rock

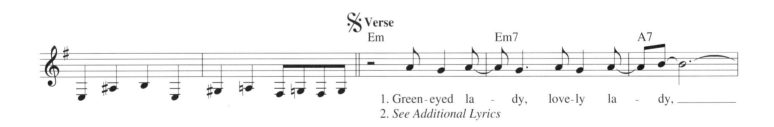

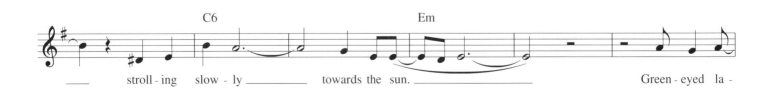

1. Green-eyed la - dy, love-ly la - dy,
2. *See Additional Lyrics*

____ stroll-ing slow-ly _____ towards the sun. _____ Green-eyed la -

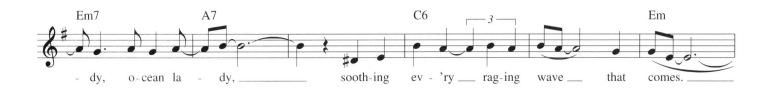

-dy, o-cean la - dy, _____ sooth-ing ev-'ry rag-ing wave _ that comes. _____

Chorus

_ Green - eyed la - dy, pas-sion's la - dy, _____ dressed in love _____ she lives _

_ for life _ to be. _____ Green-eyed la - dy feels _ life I nev - er

see set - ting sons _____ and lone-ly lov - ers free. _____

Interlude

To Coda ⊕

D.S. al Coda

⊕ *Coda*

Additional Lyrics

2. Green-eyed lady, wind-swept lady,
   Rules the night, the waves, the sand.
   Green-eyed lady, ocean lady,
   Child of nature, friend of man.

Heat of the Moment

Words and Music by Geoffrey Downes and John Wetton

*Strum Pattern: 7
*Pick Pattern: 9

* Use Pattern 3 for 4/4 measures.

1. I nev-er meant to be so bad __ to you, one thing I said that I would nev-er do. A look from you and I would fall __ from grace, and that would wipe the smile right from __ my face. _____

2. Do you re-mem-ber when we used __ to dance, and in-ci-dents a-rose from cir-cum-stance? One thing led to an-oth-er. We __ were young. And we would scream to-geth-er songs __ un-sung. _____

3., 4. See Additional Lyrics

Additional Lyrics

3. And now you find yourself in eighty-two.
   Those disco hot-spots hold no charm for you.
   You can concern yourself with bigger things.
   You catch the pearl and ride the dragon's wings.

4. And when your looks have gone and you're alone,
   How many nights you'd sit alone beside the phone.
   What were the things you wanted for yourself?
   Teenage ambitions you remember well.

Hey Joe

Words and Music by Billy Roberts

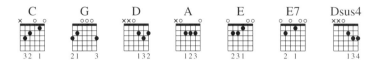

Strum Pattern: 3
Pick Pattern: 3

Verse
Moderately Slow

1. Hey _____ Joe, ___ uh, where you go - in' with that
2., 3. *See Additional Lyrics*

gun in your hand? Hey _____ Joe,

I said, where you go-in' with that gun in your hand? __ Al - right.

I'm go - in' down to shoot my old la - dy, __

you know I caught her mess-in' round with an - oth - er man.

Yeah! I'm go - in' down to shoot my old la - dy,

you bet - ter run ____ on ___ down!   Good - bye ev - 'ry - bod - y.

Ow!   Hey, ____   hey ____   Joe, ____   what'd I

Repeat and Fade

say,   run _____ on down!

Additional Lyrics

2. Uh, hey Joe, I heard you shot your woman down, you shot her down now.
   Uh, hey Joe, I heard you shot your old lady down, you shot her down in the ground. Yeah!
   Yes I did, I shot her, you know I caught her messin' 'round, messin' 'round town.
   Uh, yes I did, I shot her, you know I caught my old lady messin' 'round town.
   And I gave her the gun, I shot her!

3. Hey Joe, said now, uh, where you gonna run to now, where you gonna run to? Yeah.
   Hey Joe, I said, where you gonna run to now, where you, where you gonna go?
   Well dig it! I'm goin' way down south, way down to Mexico way. Alright!
   I'm goin' way down south, way down where I can be free.
   Ain't no one gonna find me babe!

It's Still Rock and Roll to Me

Words and Music by Billy Joel

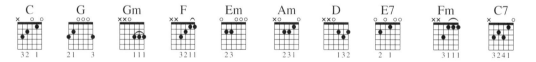

Strum Pattern: 1
Pick Pattern: 2

1. What's the mat - ter with the
2., 3., 4. *See Additional Lyrics*

clothes I'm wear-ing? Can't you tell that your tie's too wide. ____   May - be I should buy some

old tab col-lars. Wel-come back to the age of jive. _____ Where have you been hid-in'

out late-ly hon-ey? You can't dress trash-y till you spend a lot of mon-ey.

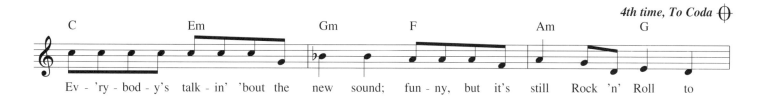

4th time, To Coda

Ev - 'ry - bod - y's talk-in' 'bout the new sound; fun-ny, but it's still Rock 'n' Roll to

Bridge

me. Oh, it does-n't mat-ter what they say in the pa-pers, 'cause it's

al-ways been the same old scene. There's a new band in town but you can't get the sound from a

D.S. al Coda
(take repeat)

sto - ry in a mag - a - zine aimed _ at your av - er - age teen.

Coda

Outro

me. Ev - 'ry-bod - y's talk-in' 'bout the new sound; fun-ny, but it's still Rock 'n' Roll to me.

Additional Lyrics

2. What's the matter with the car I'm driving? Can't you tell that it's out of style.
Should I get a set of whitewall tires? Are you gonna cruise the Miracle Mile?
Nowadays you can't be too sentimental. Your best bet's a true baby blue Continental.
Hot funk, cool punk, even if it's old junk, it's still Rock 'n' Roll to me.

3. How about a pair of pink sidewinders and a bright orange pair of pants?
Well, you could really be a Beau Brummel baby, if you just give it half a chance.
Don't waste your money on a new set of speakers. You get more mileage from a cheap pair of sneakers.
Next phase, new wave, dance craze; anyways it's still Rock 'n' Roll to me.

4. What's the matter with the crowd I'm seeing? Don't you know that they're out of touch?
Should I try to be a straight "A" student? If you are then you think too much.
Don't you know about the new fashion honey? All you need are looks and a whole lot of money.
It's the next phase, new wave, dance craze; anyways it's still Rock 'n' Roll to me.

I Shot the Sheriff

Words and Music by Bob Marley

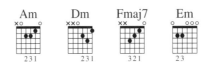

Strum Pattern: 3
Pick Pattern: 3

Additional Lyrics

2. Sheriff John Brown always hated me;
   For what, I don't know.
   And every time that I plant a seed,
   He said, "Kill it before it grows,"
   "Kill it before it grows."

3. Freedom came my way one day,
   So I started out of town.
   All of a sudden, I see Sheriff Brown
   Aimin' to shoot me down,
   So I shot him down.

4. Reflexes got the better of me,
   What will be will be.
   Everyday, the bucket goes to the well,
   One day the bottom will drop out
   I say, one day the bottom will drop out.

I Want to Hold Your Hand

Words and Music by John Lennon and Paul McCartney

Strum Pattern: 6
Pick Pattern: 3

Additional Lyrics

2. Oh, please say to me
   You'll let me be your man.
   And please say to me
   You'll let me hold your hand.

3. Yeah, you got that something
   I think you'll understand.
   When I feel that something
   I want to hold your hand.

MCA Music Publishing

I Want You to Want Me

Words and Music by Rick Nielsen

Strum Pattern: 4
Pick Pattern: 1

𝄋 **Chorus**

Additional Lyrics

Chorus 2. I want you to want me.
     I need you to need me.
     I'd love you to love me.

Jailbreak

Words and Music by Philip Parris Lynott

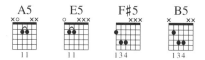

Strum Pattern: 5
Pick Pattern: 6

Intro
Moderately

1. To -

Verse

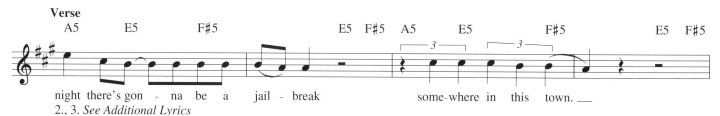

night there's gon - na be a jail - break   some-where in this town. __
2., 3. *See Additional Lyrics*

See, me and the boys __ we don't like it,   so we're get-tin' up and go-in' down. __

Hid-in' low,   look-in' right to left. __   If you see us com-in' I think it's __ best

to move a-way.   Do you hear what I   say,   from un-der my breath?   To -

Chorus

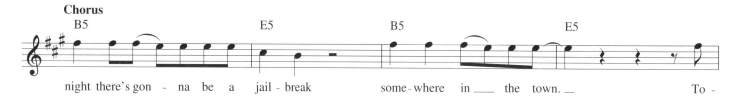

night there's gon - na be a jail - break   some-where in __ the town. __   To -

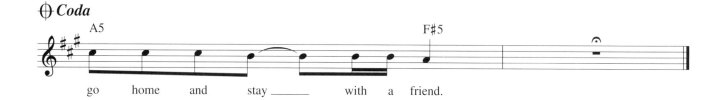

Coda

A5   F#5

go   home   and   stay ____ with   a   friend.

Additional Lyrics

2. Tonight there's gonna be trouble.
   Some of us won't survive.
   See, the boys and me mean business.
   Bustin' out dead or alive.
   I can hear hound dogs on my trail.
   All hell breaks loose, alarm and sirens wail.
   Like a game, if you lose go to jail!

3. Tonight there's gonna be a breakout,
   Into the city zones.
   Don't you dare try to stop us,
   No one could for long.
   Searchlight on my trail.
   Tonight's the night, all systems fail.
   Good lookin' female, come here.

Jessie's Girl

Words and Music by Rick Springfield

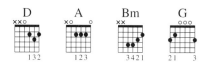

D   A   Bm   G

Strum Pattern: 1
Pick Pattern: 2

Intro
Fast

D   A   Bm   G   A   D   A   Bm   G

Verse

A   D   D   A   Bm   G   A   D

1. Jes - sie   is   a   friend,   yeah,   I   know
2. See Additional Lyrics

A   Bm   G   A   D   A   Bm

____ he's   been   a   good   friend   of   mine. ____   But   late - ly   some-thing's changed;_ it   ain't   hard_

Additional Lyrics

2. I'll play along with this charade.
   There doesn't seem to be a reason to change.
   You know, I feel so dirty when they start talkin' cute.
   I wanna tell her that I love her, but the point is prob'ly moot.

Jesus Is Just Alright

Words and Music by Arthur Reynolds

* Strum Pattern: 6
* Pick Pattern: 5

Intro
Bright Rock

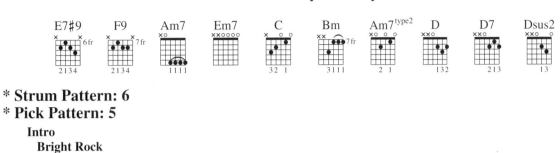

Do, do, do, do, _ do, do, _ do, do. _   Do, do, do, do, _ do, do, _ do, do. _

* Use Pattern 8 for ¾ measures.

Do, do, do, do, _ do, do, _ do, do. _   Do, do, do, do, _ do, do. _

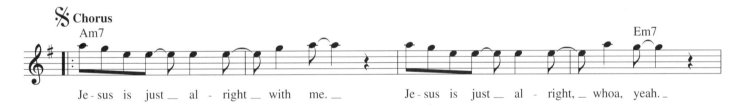

Je - sus is just _ al - right _ with me. _   Je - sus is just _ al - right, _ whoa, yeah. _

Je - sus is just _ al - right _ with me. _   Je - sus is just _ al - right. _

I don't care _ what they _ may { say. _ / know. _ / say. _ }   I don't care _ { what / where / what } they _

_ may { do. _ / go. _ / do. _ }   I don't care _ what they _ may { say. _ / know. _ / say. _ }   Je - sus is just _ al - right,

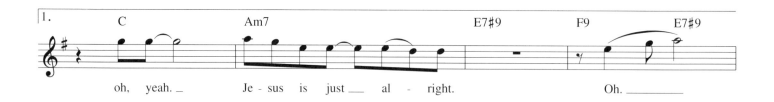

oh, yeah. ___ Je - sus is just ___ al - right. Oh. _____

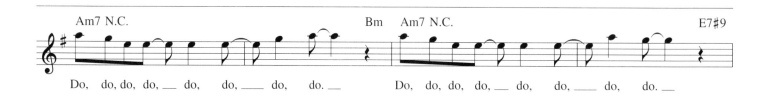

Do, do, do, do, ___ do, do, ___ do, do. ___ Do, do, do, do, ___ do, do, ___ do, do. ___

Do, do, do, do, ___ do, do, ___ do, do. ___ Do, do, do, do, ___ do, do. _____ A

hop - in' and a - pray - in'. _____ oh, yeah. _

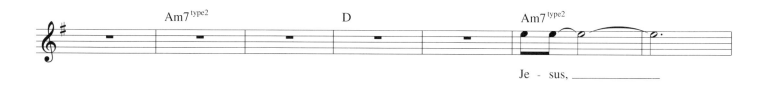

Je - sus, _____

he's my ___ friend. ___
Instrumental
Je - sus, _____

___ well, he's my _____ friend. _____

He took me by the hand, ___ lead me far ___

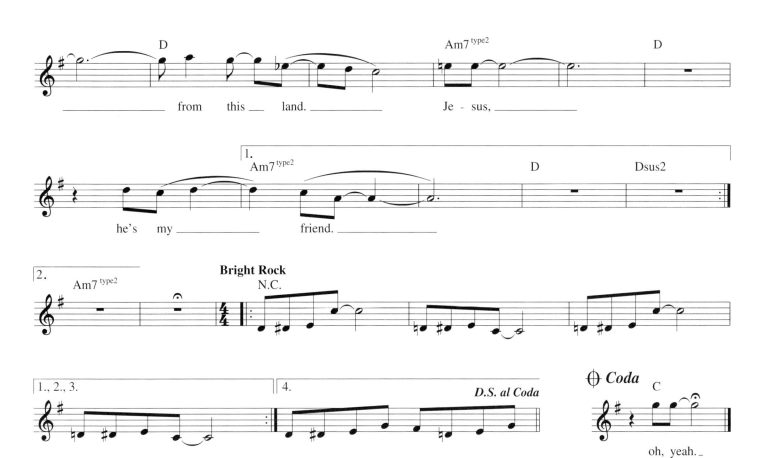

from this land. Je - sus,

1. he's my friend.

2. | **Bright Rock** N.C.

1., 2., 3. | **4.** *D.S. al Coda* | ⊕ *Coda*

oh, yeah.

Leave It

Words and Music by Trevor Horn, Trevor Rabin and Chris Squire

C7 F C Dm B♭ Gm G G7 Cm

* Strum Pattern: 4
* Pick Pattern: 1

Intro
Moderately
N.C.

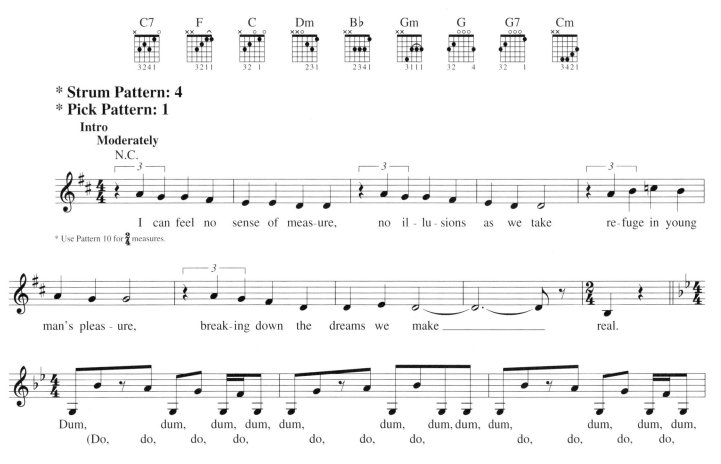

I can feel no sense of meas-ure, no il - lu - sions as we take re-fuge in young

* Use Pattern 10 for 2/4 measures.

man's pleas - ure, break-ing down the dreams we make real.

Dum, dum, dum, dum, dum, dum, dum, dum, dum, dum, dum, dum,
(Do, do, do, do, do, do, do, do, do, do, do,

dum,   dum,   dum, dum, dum,   dum,   dum, dum, dum,   dum, dum, dum,

do,   do,   do,   do,   do,   do,   do,   do,   do,

Verse
N.C.

dum,   dum, dum, dum,   dum.

do,   do,   do,   do,   do,   do,   do.)

1. One down, one to go; an -
2. *See Additional Lyrics*

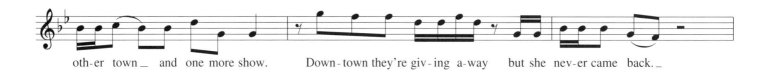

oth-er town   and one more show.   Down-town they're giv-ing a-way   but she nev-er came back.

No phone can take your place; you know what I mean.   We have the same in-trigue as a

Chorus
C7   F C Dm C F C7   F   C   Dm

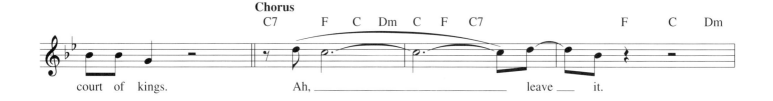

court of kings.   Ah, _____ leave ___ it.

C F C7   F C Dm C   F C7   F   C   Dm C F C7

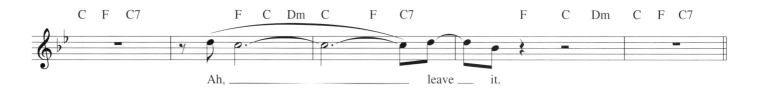

Ah, _____ leave ___ it.

| 1. | 2. |

     Bridge

C7 F   C   Dm   C   F   C7   N.C.

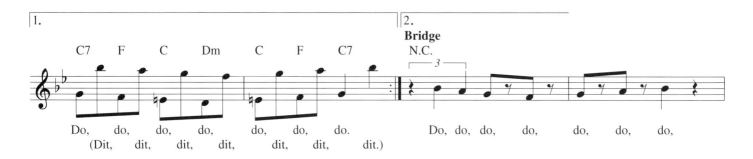

Do, do, do, do,   do,   do,   do.   Do, do, do, do,   do,   do,   do,

(Dit, dit, dit, dit,   dit,   dit,   dit.)

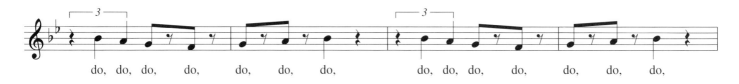

do, do, do, do,   do,   do,   do,   do, do, do, do,   do,   do,   do,

Additional Lyrics

2. Two down, there you go. MacArthur Park in the driving snow.
Uptown they're digging out; better lay your claim.
Get home; you're not alone. You just broke out of the danger zone.
Be there to show your face on another dreamy day.

Juke Box Hero

Words and Music by Mick Jones and Lou Gramm

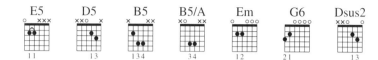

Strum Pattern: 4
Pick Pattern: 6

Verse
Moderate Rock (♪♪ = ♪♪)

1. Stand-in' in the rain ___ with his head hung low.

Could-n't get a tick-et. It was a sold-out show.

Heard the roar of the crowd. He could pic-ture the scene. ___

Put his ear to the wall. Then, like a dis-tant scream,

he heard one gui-tar. ___ Just blew him a-way.

Saw stars in his eyes. And the ver-y next day, bought a beat-up

six-string in a sec-ond-hand store. Did-n't know how to play it,

but he knew ___ for sure. That one gui-tar ___ felt good in his

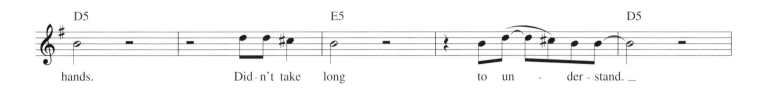
hands. Did-n't take long to un - der - stand. ___

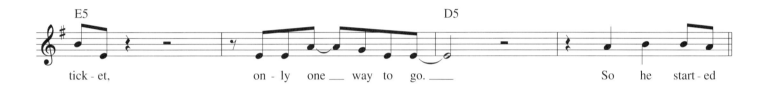
Just one gui-tar ___ slung way down low was a one - way

tick - et, on - ly one ___ way to go. ___ So he start-ed

𝄋 Pre-Chorus

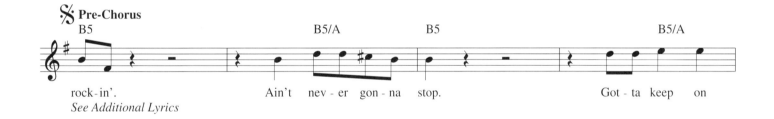
rock-in'.
See Additional Lyrics
Ain't nev - er gon - na stop. Got - ta keep on

rock - in'. Some - day he's gon - na make it to the top. ___ And be a

Chorus

juke - box he - ro. (Got stars in his ___ eyes.) He's a juke - box

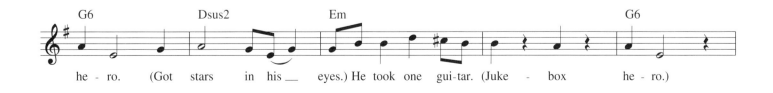
he - ro. (Got stars in his ___ eyes.) He took one gui-tar. (Juke - box he - ro.)

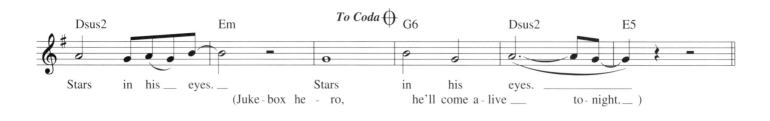

Stars in his __ eyes. __ Stars in his eyes. __
(Juke - box he - ro, he'll come a - live __ to - night. __)

Interlude

2. In a town with - out a

Verse

name. In a heav - y down - pour. Thought he passed his own

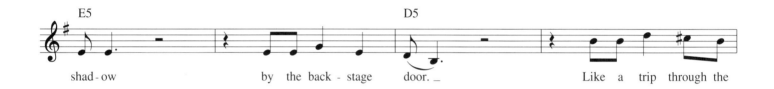

shad - ow by the back - stage door. __ Like a trip through the

past, that day in the rain, that one gui - tar __

D.S. al Coda

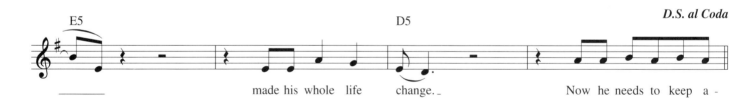

__ made his whole life change. _ Now he needs to keep a -

⊕ *Coda*

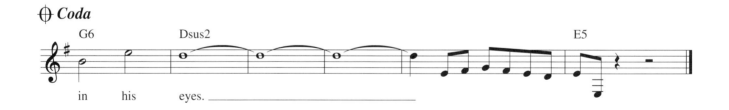

in his eyes. _____

Additional Lyrics

Pre-Chorus Now he needs to keep a-rockin'.
He just can't stop. Gotta keep on rockin'.
That boy has got to stay on top.

Love Stinks

Words and Music by Seth Justman and Peter Wolf

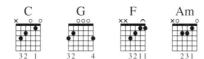

Strum Pattern: 6
Pick Pattern: 5

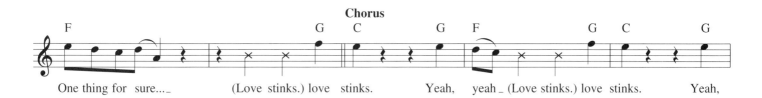

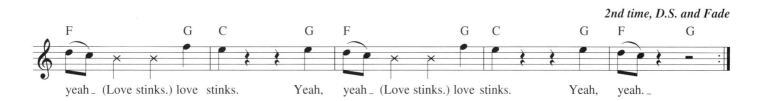

Additional Lyrics

2. Two by two, and side by side,
   Love's gonna find you, yes it is.
   You just can't hide. You'll hear it call; your heart will fall.
   Then love will fly. It's gone that's all.

Killer Queen

Words and Music by Freddie Mercury

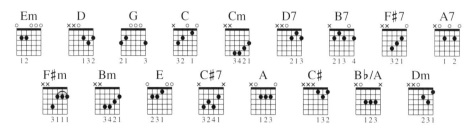

Em   D   G   C   Cm   D7   B7   F#7   A7

F#m   Bm   E   C#7   A   C#   Bb/A   Dm

* Strum Pattern: 3
* Pick Pattern: 3

Moderate Rock   **Verse**

1. She keeps __ Mo - et and Chan - don in her pret - ty cab - i - net,
2. *See Additional Lyrics*

* Use Pattern 10 for ⅔ measures and Pattern 8 for ⅜ measures.

"Let them eat cake," she says, just like Ma - rie An - toin - ette. A built - in rem - e - dy for

Khru - shchev and Ken - ne - dy, and an - y time an in - vi - ta - tion you can de - cline. __

Cav - i - ar and cig - a - rettes, well versed in et - i - quette, ex - tr'or - di - nar - i - ly nice. She's a

Chorus

kill - er queen, __ gun pow - der, gel - a - tine, dy - na - mite with a la - ser beam,

guar - an - teed to blow your mind, __ an - y time, ooh. Rec - om - mend - ed at the price, in -

To Coda

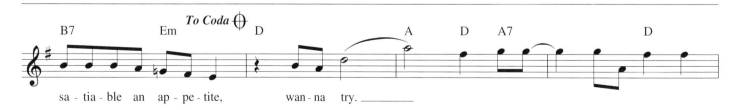

sa - tia - ble an ap - pe - tite, wan - na try. _____

Additional Lyrics

2. To avoid complications, she never kept the same address.
   In conversation she spoke just like a baroness.
   Met a man from China, went down to Geisha Minah,
   Then again, incidentally, if you're that way inclined.
   Perfume came nat'rally from Paris.
   For cars she couldn't care less. Fastidious and precise.

Long Cool Woman (In a Black Dress)

Words and Music by Allan Clarke, Roger Cook and Roger Greenaway

Additional Lyrics

2. I saw her head up to the table.
   Well, a tall walking big black cat.
   When Charlie said, "I hope that you're able."
   Boy, I'm telling you she knows where it's at.
   Suddenly we heard the sirens, and ev'rybody started to run.
   Jumpin' out of doors and tables when I heard somebody shooting a gun.

Message in a Bottle

Written and Composed by Sting

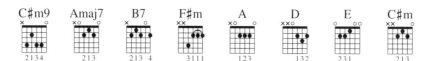

Strum Pattern: 1, 6
Pick Pattern: 2, 6

Intro
Fast

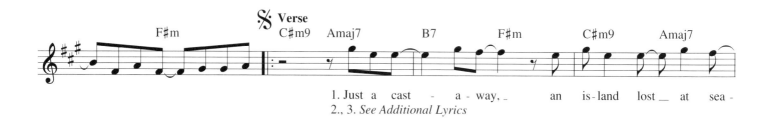

1. Just a cast - a - way, _ an is - land lost _ at sea -
2., 3. *See Additional Lyrics*

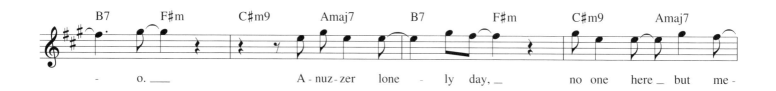

- o. ___ A - nuz - zer lone - ly day, _ no one here _ but me -

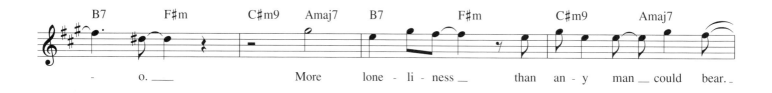

- o. ___ More lone - li - ness _ than an - y man _ could bear. _

___ Res - cue me _ be - fore _ I fall _ in - to _ des - pair -

Chorus

- o. ___ I'll send _ an S. _ O. S. _ to the world. _ I'll send _ an S. _

_____ O. _____ S. _____ to the world. _____ I hope _ that some - one gets _ my, _____ I hope _ that some -

- one gets _ my, _____ I hope _ that some - one gets _ my mes-sage in _____ a bot -

To Coda

- tle, _____ yeah. Mes-sage in _____ a bot - tle, _____ yeah.

1. / 2.

D.S. al Coda

Coda

Outro

Mes - sage in _____ a bot - tle. _____

Mes - sage in _____ a bot - tle, _____ oh, yeah.

Repeat and Fade

I'm send - ing out _____ an S. _____ O. _____ S. _____ I'm

Additional Lyrics

2. A year has passed since I wrote my note,
But I should have known this right from the start.
Only hope can keep me together.
Love can mend your life but love can break your heart.

3. Walked out this morning, I don't believe what I saw.
A hundred billion bottles washed up on the shore.
Seems like I'm not alone in being alone.
A hundred billion castaways looking for a home.

Low Rider

Words and Music by Sylvester Allen, Harold R. Brown, Morris Dickerson, Jerry Goldstein, Leroy Jordan, Lee Oskar, Charles W. Miller and Howard Scott

Strum Pattern: 3, 6
Pick Pattern: 3, 6

Intro
Moderately

Verse

1. All my friends know the low rid-er.
2., 3., 4. *See Additional Lyrics*

The low rid - er is a lit-tle high-er.

Interlude

play 4 times

Outro

Take a lit-tle trip, take a lit-tle trip, take a lit-tle trip { and see. / with me.

Additional Lyrics

2. Low rider drives a little slower.
   Low rider he's a real goer.

3. Low rider knows ev'ry street, yeah.
   Low rider is the one to meet, yeah.

4. Low rider don't use no gas, now.
   Low rider don't drive too fast.

No Particular Place to Go

Words and Music by Chuck Berry

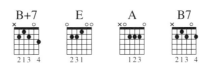

Strum Pattern: 1
Pick Pattern: 2

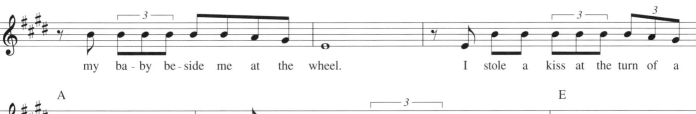

1. Rid - ing a - long in my au - to - mo - bile,

2., 3., 4. See Additional Lyrics

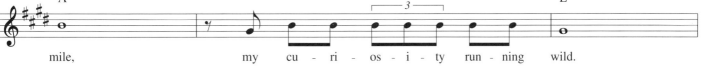

my ba - by be - side me at the wheel. I stole a kiss at the turn of a

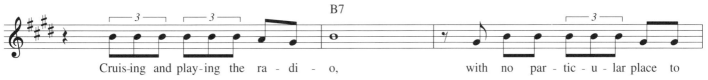

mile, my cu - ri - os - i - ty run - ning wild.

Cruis-ing and play-ing the ra - di - o, with no par - tic - u - lar place to

1., 2., 3.   **4.**

go.   2. Rid - ing a - long in my au - to - mo-   go.

Additional Lyrics

2. Riding along in my automobile,
   I was anxious to tell her the way I feel.
   So I told her softly and sincere
   And she leaned and whispered in my ear.
   Cuddling more and driving slow,
   With no particular place to go.

3. No particular place to go,
   So we parked way out on the cocamo.
   The night was young and the moon was gold,
   So we both decided to take a stroll.
   Can you image the way I felt?
   I couldn't unfasten her safety belt.

4. Riding along in my calaboose,
   Still trying to get her belt unloose.
   All the way home I held a grudge,
   For the safety belt that wouldn't budge.
   Crusing and playing the radio,
   With no particular place to go.

Money for Nothing

Words and Music by Mark Knopfler and Sting

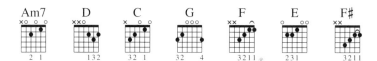

Strum Pattern: 2
Pick Pattern: 4

Intro
Moderate Rock

𝄋 Verse

1., 6. Look at them _ yo - yos.   That's _ the way to do it. _   Play the gui - tar on the
4. *See Additional Lyrics*

M.   T.   V.   That ain't _ work - in'.   That's _ the way to do it.

To Coda ⊕
Verse

Mon - ey   for noth - in' and   chicks for free. _   2. That ain't work - in'.   That's _
3., 5. *See Additional Lyrics*

_ the way you do it.   Lem - me tell ya   them _ guys ain't dumb. _

Am7

May - be get a blis - ter on your lit - tle fin - ger. May - be get a

Chorus

G   Am7   F   C

blis - ter on your __ thumb. __ We got - ta in - stall mi - cro - wave ov - ens,

F   G   Am7

cust - om kit - chen de - liv - er - ies. _____ We got - ta move these

2nd time, D.S.
3rd time, D.S. al Coda

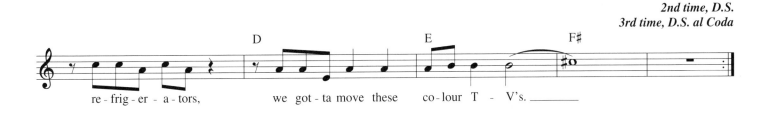

D   E   F♯

re - frig - er - a - tors, we got - ta move these co - lour T - V's. _____

⊕ *Coda*

Outro

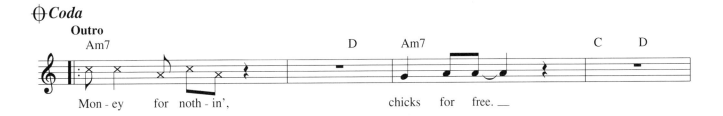

Am7   D   Am7   C   D

Mon - ey for noth - in', chicks for free. __

Repeat and Fade

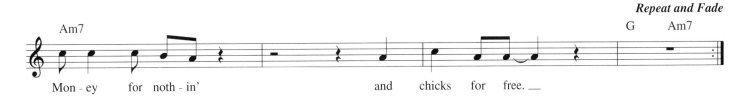

Am7   G   Am7

Mon - ey for noth - in' and chicks for free. __

Additional Lyrics

3. See that little faggot with the earring and the makeup.
   Yeah, buddy, that's his own hair.
   That little faggot got his own jet airplane.
   That little faggot he's a millionaire.

4. I shoulda learned to play the guitar.
   I shoulda learned to play them drums.
   Look at that, she got it stickin' in the camera.
   Man, we could have some fun.

5. And he's up there he's making Hawaiian noises,
   Bangin' on the the bongos like a chimpanzee.
   That ain't workin'. That's the way you do it.
   Money for nothin' and chicks for free.

Miss You

Words and Music by Mick Jagger and Keith Richards

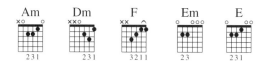

Strum Pattern: 1
Pick Pattern: 2

Verse
Moderately

I've been hold-ing out so long, I've been sleep-ing all a-lone, Lord I miss you.

I've been hang-ing on the phone, I've been sleep-ing all a-lone, I want to kiss you. Hoo, hoo,

Chorus

hoo, _ hoo, _____ hoo, hoo, hoo, _ hoo, _____ hoo, hoo, hoo, hoo. _ Hoo, hoo,

2.

Verse

2. Well, I've been haunt-ed in my sleep, _ you've been star-ring in my dreams, Lord I

miss you child. _ I've been wait-ing in the hall, been wait-ing on your call. When the

phone rings, *Spoken:* It's just some friends of mine that say, "Hey, *what's the matter man? We're gonna come around at twelve o'clock*

with some Puerto Rican girls that are just dyin' to meet you. We're gonna bring a case of wine, hey, let's go mess and fool around,

4. I guess I'm ly-ing to my-self, it's just you and no one else, Lord I

won't miss you child. _____ You've just been blot-ting out my mind,

fool - ing on my time, no I won't miss you ba - by. _____ Lord, _

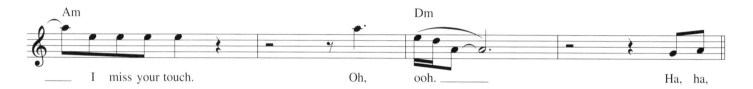

_____ I miss your touch. Oh, ooh. _____ Ha, ha,

ha, ha, ha, _ ha, _____ ha, ha, ha, ha, ha, _ ha, _____ ha, ha, ha, ha. _____ Ha, ha,

Paperback Writer

Words and Music by John Lennon and Paul McCartney

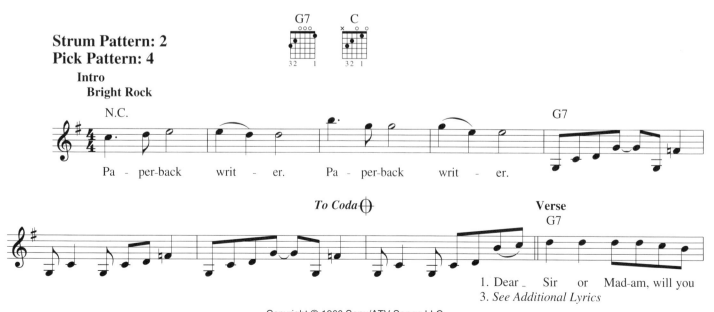

Strum Pattern: 2
Pick Pattern: 4

Intro
Bright Rock

Pa - per-back writ - er. Pa - per-back writ - er.

1. Dear _ Sir or Mad-am, will you
3. *See Additional Lyrics*

read my book? It took me years to write, — will you take a look? It's

based on a nov - el by a man named Lear and I need a job ___ so I

want to be a pa - per - back writ - er, _____ pa - per - back writ - er. _____

Verse

_____ 2. It's the dirt - y sto - ry of a dirt - y man _ and his cling - ing wife _ does - n't
4. *See Additional Lyrics*

un - der - stand. His son is work - ing for the Dai - ly Mail. _ It's a stead - y job, _ but he

wants to be a pa - per - back writ - er, _____ pa - per - back writ - er. _____

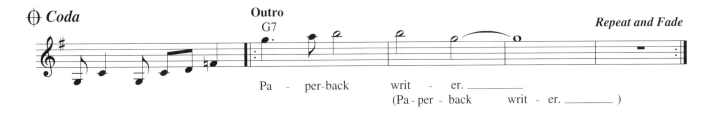

Pa - per - back writ - er. _____
(Pa - per - back writ - er. _____)

Additional Lyrics

3. It's a thousand pages, give or take a few;
   I'll be writing more in a week or two.
   I can make it longer if you like the style,
   I can change it 'round, and I want to be a paperback writer,
   Paperback writer.

4. If you really like it you can have the rights;
   It could make a million for you overnight.
   If you must return it you can send it here,
   But I need a break and I want to be a paperback writer,
   Paperback writer.

New Kid in Town

Words and Music by John David Souther, Don Henley and Glenn Frey

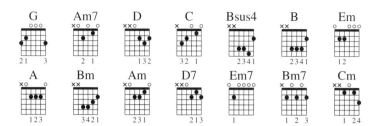

Strum Pattern: 3, 6
Pick Pattern: 3, 5

Intro
Moderately

Verse

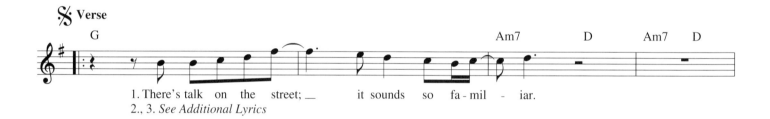

1. There's talk on the street; __ it sounds so fa - mil - iar.
2., 3. *See Additional Lyrics*

Great ex - pec - ta - tions, ev - 'ry - bod - y's watch - ing you. __

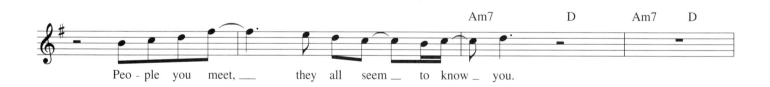

Peo - ple you meet, __ they all seem __ to know __ you.

To Coda

E - ven your old ____ friends treat you like you're some - thing new. __

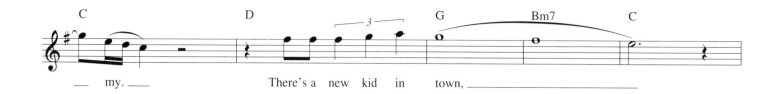

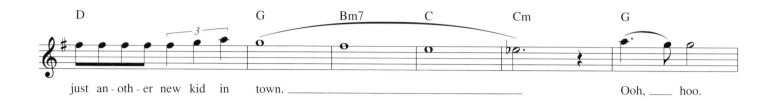

Additional Lyrics

2. You look in her eyes; the music begins to play.
   Hopeless romantics, here we go again.
   But after awhile you're looking the other way.
   It's those restless hearts that never mend.

3. There's talk on the street; it's there to remind you
   That it doesn't really matter which side you're on.
   You're walking away and they're talking behind you.
   They will never forget you till somebody new comes along.

Not Fade Away

Words and Music by Charles Hardin and Norman Petty

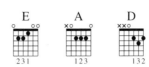

Strum Pattern: 2
Pick Pattern: 4

Additional Lyrics

2. My love is bigger than a Cadillac.
   I try to show it and you drive me back.
   Your love for me got to be real,
   For you to know-a just how I feel.
   A love for real'll not fade away.

3. I'm a-gonna tell you how it's gonna be.
   You're gonna give-a your love to me.
   A love to last more than one day.
   A love that's love'll not fade away.
   A love that's love'll not fade away.

Oh, Pretty Woman

Words and Music by Roy Orbison and Bill Dees

*Strum Pattern: 2
*Pick Pattern: 4

Additional Lyrics

2. Pretty woman, won't you pardon me?
Pretty woman, I couldn't help but see;
Pretty woman, that you look lovely as can be.
Are you lonely just like me?

Paranoid

Words and Music by Anthony Iommi, John Osbourne, William Ward and Terence Butler

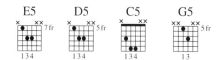

Strum Pattern: 1
Pick Pattern: 2

Intro
Hard Rock

1. Fin-ished with _ my wom - an 'cause _ she could-n't help _ me with my mind.
4. *See Additional Lyrics*

Peo - ple think _ I'm in - sane be - cause I am frown - ing all the time.

Interlude

Verse

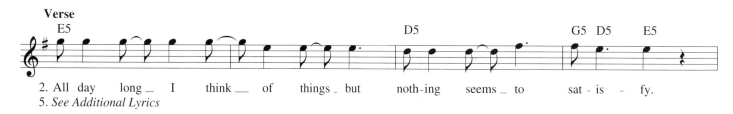

2. All day long _ I think _ of things _ but noth-ing seems _ to sat - is - fy.
5. *See Additional Lyrics*

To Coda ⊕

Think I'll lose _ my mind _ if I _ don't find some - thing _ to pac - i - fy.

Bridge

Can you help _ me?   Are __ you __ for __ my __ brain?

__   Oh _____ yeah. __

Interlude

Verse

3. I need some - one to __ show me __ the things in life __ that I can't find.

D.S. al Coda

I can't see __ the things _ that make _ true hap - pi - ness, _ I must be blind.

⊕ *Coda*
Outro   *Repeat and Fade*

Additional Lyrics

4. Make a joke and I will sigh
   And you will laugh and I will cry.
   Happiness I cannot feel
   So love to me is so unreal.

5. And so as you hear these words
   Telling you now of my state.
   I tell you to enjoy life,
   I wish I could but it's too late.

Peace of Mind

Words and Music by Tom Scholz

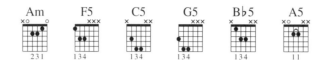

Strum Pattern: 1, 3
Pick Pattern: 2, 3

Intro
Moderate Rock

1. Now, if you're feel-in' kind-a low 'bout the
2., 3. *See Additional Lyrics*

dues you been pay - in', fu - ture's com - in' much too ___ slow. ___ And you

wan - na run but some-how you just keep on stay - in', can't de - cide on which way to go, _

___ whoa. _ Yeah, yeah, yeah! I un - der - stand _ a - bout in - de - ci - sion, _ but

I don't care _ if I get be - hind. _ Peo - ple liv - ing in com - pe - ti - tion.

Additional Lyrics

2. Now, you're climin' to the top of the company ladder,
   Hope it doesn't take too long.
   Can't you see there'll come a day when it won't matter,
   Come a day when you'll be gone. Whoa!

3. Now, ev'rybody's got advice they just keep on givin',
   Doesn't mean too much to me.
   Lots of people have to make believe they're livin',
   Can't decide who they should be. Whoa!

Pictures of Lily

Words and Music by Peter Townshend

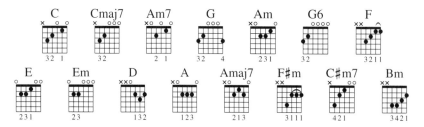

Strum Pattern: 3
Pick Pattern: 3

Verse
Moderately

1. I used to wake up in the morn-ings, _ I used to feel so bad. __
2. *See Additional Lyrics*

I got so sick of hav-ing sleep-less nights. _ I went and told my dad. _

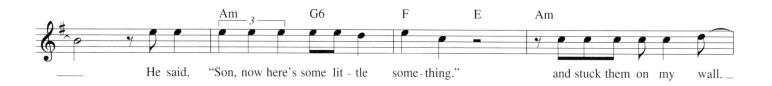

___ He said, "Son, now here's some lit-tle some-thing." and stuck them on my wall. _

__ And now my nights ain't quite so lone-ly, in fact I I don't feel bad at all, _

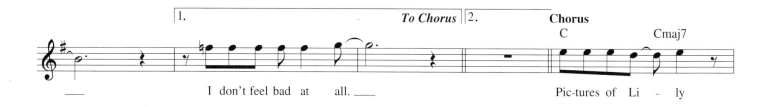

1.
___ I don't feel bad at all. __

To Chorus 2. **Chorus**

Pic-tures of Li - ly

made my life __ so won - der - ful. __ Pic-tures of Li - ly helped _

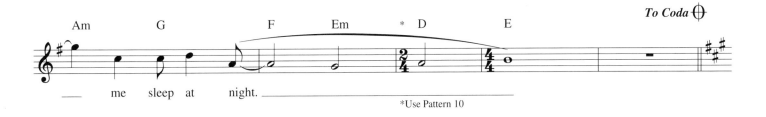

me sleep at night. _____

*Use Pattern 10

Chorus

Pic - tures of Li - ly, solved my child - hood prob - lems.

Pic - tures of Li - ly, helped me feel al - right. _____

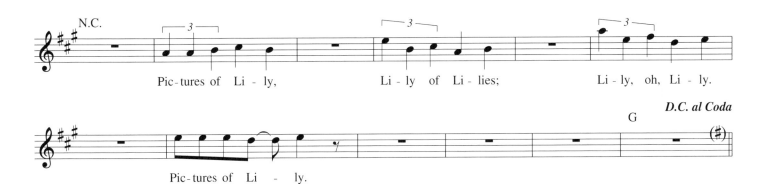

Pic - tures of Li - ly, Li - ly of Li - lies; Li - ly, oh, Li - ly.

D.C. al Coda

Pic - tures of Li - ly.

Coda
Outro

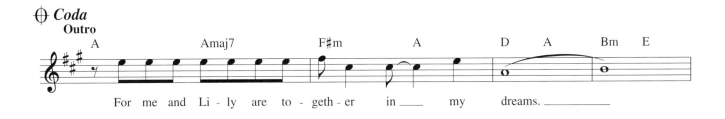

For me and Li - ly are to - geth - er in ___ my dreams. _____

And I ask you, hey Mis - ter have you ev - er seen ___ pic - tures of Li - ly?

Additional Lyrics

2. And then one day things weren't quite so fine.
I fell in love with Lily.
I asked my dad where Lily I could find.
He said, "Son, now don't be silly.
She's been dead since nineteen twenty-nine."
Oh, how I cried that night!
If only I'd been born in Lily's time,
It would have been alright.

Piece of My Heart

Words and Music by Jerry Ragovoy and Bert Berns

Verse

out in the street look - in' good, ____ and you know ____ deep down

in your heart that ain't right. ____ And oh, you

nev - er, nev - er hear me when I cry at night. _ Whoa, oh, oh,

____ I tell my - self ____ that I can't stand the pain. But when you

hold me in your arms I say it a - gain. _ So go on, go on,

D.S. al Coda   ⊕ *Coda*

go on, go on,   You know you got it if it makes you feel good. _

Pride and Joy

By Stevie Ray Vaughan

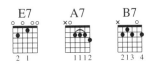

Strum Pattern: 3
Pick Pattern: 3

Verse
Moderate Blues Shuffle

1. Well, you've heard a - bout love giv - in' sight ____ to the blind.

My ba - by's lov - in' cause the sun to shine. _ She's my sweet lit - tle thing, _

she's my pride and joy. ____ She's my

sweet lit - tle ba - by, I'm ___ her ___ lit - tle lov - er boy. _____

Verse

2. Yeah, I love my la - dy to be long and lean, ___
3., 4. *See Additional Lyrics*

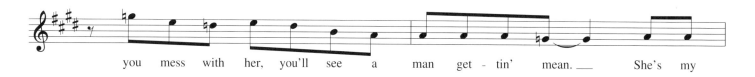

you mess with her, you'll see a man get - tin' mean. ___ She's my

sweet lit - tle thing, ___ she's my pride and joy. ___

She's my sweet lit - tle ba - by, I'm ___ her ___ lit - tle lov - er

boy. _____ 3. Yeah, I 4. Yeah, I

Additional Lyrics

3. Yeah, I love my baby like the finest wine;
Stick with her until the end of time.
She's my sweet little thing,
She's my pride and joy.
She's my sweet little baby,
I'm her little lover boy.

4. Yeah, I love my baby, my heart and soul;
Love like ours won't never grow old.
She's my sweet little thing,
She's my pride and joy.
She's my sweet little baby,
I'm her little lover boy.

Rhiannon

Words and Music by Stevie Nicks

Strum Pattern: 1
Pick Pattern: 2

Intro
Moderately

Em · C

1. Rhi -

Verse

Em · C

an - non rings _ like a bell thru the night, and would-n't you love to love _ her? _
2. *See Additional Lyrics*

Em · C

Takes to the sky like a bird in flight _ and who will be _ her lov - er?

Bridge

G · C

All your life _ you've nev - er seen _ a wom-an _ tak - en by the wind. _

G · C

Would you stay _ if she prom - ised you heav-en? Will you ev - er win? _

Chorus

C · Em · Em · C · Em · *play 4 times*

Will you ev - er win? _ Rhi - an - non.

Outro · *Repeat and Fade*

Em9 · Em · C

Dreams un - wind; love's _ a state of mind. _

Additional Lyrics

2. She is like a cat in the dark,
   And then she is the darkness.
   She rules her life like a fine skylark,
   And when the sky is starless.

Pretending

Words and Music by Jerry Williams

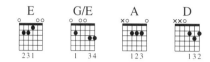

E   G/E   A   D

Strum Pattern: 3
Pick Pattern: 3

Verse
Moderately Slow

1. How man-y times _ must we tell the tale? _ How man-y times _ must we fall?

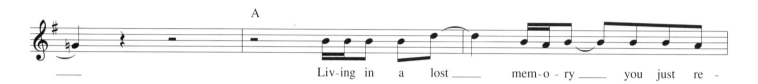

_ Liv-ing in a lost _ mem-o-ry _ you just re -

called. _ 2. Work-ing on _ the sound of the band, _
3., 4. *See Additional Lyrics*

try-ing to get the mu - sic right, two go out _ work-ing,

three stay home at night. _ That's when she said she was pre -

tend-ing, like she knew the plan. _ That's when I knew she was pre -

tend-ing, pre - tend-ing to un - der-stand. _ Pre -

Additional Lyrics

3. Satisfied but lost in love, situations change.
   You're never who you used to think you are, how strange.

4. I get lost in alibis, sadness can't prevail.
   Everybody knows strong love can't fail.

Ramblin' Man

Words and Music by Dickey Betts

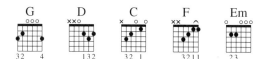

Strum Pattern: 6
Pick Pattern: 4

Intro
Fast Rock

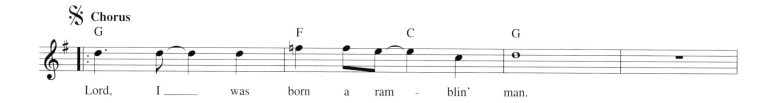

Lord, I _____ was born a ram - blin' man.

Try'n to make a liv - ing, and do - in' the best I _____ can.

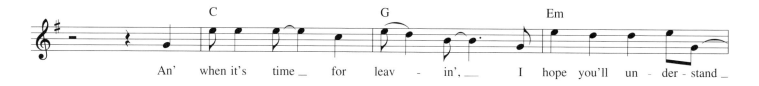

An' when it's time _ for leav - in', _ I hope you'll un - der - stand _

_____ that I was born _____ a ram - blin' man.

Verse

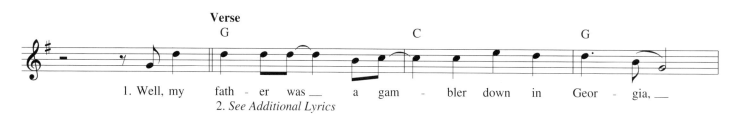

1. Well, my fath - er was _ a gam - bler down in Geor - gia, _
2. *See Additional Lyrics*

and he wound up on _ the wrong _ end of a gun. _

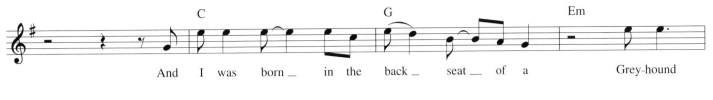

And I was born _ in the back _ seat _ of a Grey-hound

2nd time, D.S. al Coda

bus, roll - in' _ down High - way For - ty One. _

⊕ *Coda*

Outro

Lord, I _ was born a ram - blin' man. _

Repeat and Fade

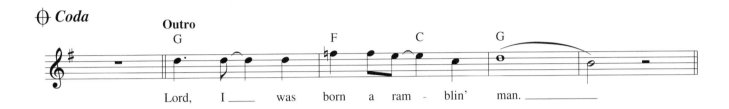

Lord, I _ was born a ram - blin' man. _

Additional Lyrics

2. I'm on my way to New Orleans this mornin',
   And leavin' out of Nashville, Tennessee.
   They're always havin' a good time down on the bayou, Lord.
   Them delta women think the world of me.

Smoke on the Water

Words and Music by Ritchie Blackmore, Ian Gillan, Roger Glover, Jon Lord and Ian Paice

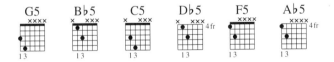

Strum Pattern: 3
Pick Pattern: 3

Intro
Moderate Rock

1. We all came out to Mon - treaux on the
2., 3. *See Additional Lyrics*

Additional Lyrics

2. They burned down the gamblin' house,
It died with an awful sound.
A-Funky Claude was running in and out,
Pulling kids out the ground.
When it all was over,
We had to find another place.
But Swiss time was running out;
It seemed that we would lose the race.

3. We ended up at the Grand Hotel,
It was empty, cold and bare.
But with the Rolling truck Stones thing just outside,
Making our music there.
With a few red lights, a few old beds,
We made a place to sweat.
No matter what we get out of this,
I know, I know we'll never forget.

Spinning Wheel

Words and Music by David Clayton Thomas

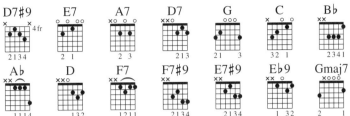

Strum Pattern: 4
Pick Pattern: 1

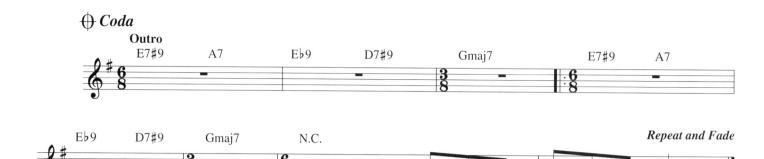

⊕ Coda

Outro

Repeat and Fade

Additional Lyrics

2. Ya' got no money and ya', ya' got no home.
   Spinnin' wheel, all alone.
   Talkin' 'bout your troubles and ya', ya' never learn.
   Ride a painted pony, let the spinnin' wheel turn.

3. Someone is waitin' just for you.
   Spinnin' wheel, spinnin' true.
   Drop all your troubles by the riverside.
   Catch a painted pony on the spinnin' wheel ride.

The Story in Your Eyes

Words and Music by Justin Hayward

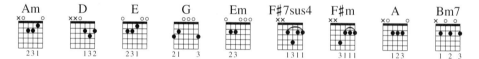

Strum Pattern: 1
Pick Pattern: 2

Intro
Fast Rock

1. I've been

𝄋 Verse

think - ing   'bout _ our   for - tune _____ and I've de - cid - ed that we're real - ly not to
fright - ened   for _ your   chil - dren. _____   And the   life that we are liv - ing is in
3. *See Additional Lyrics*

blame _____   for   the   love   that's   deep   in - side   us   now _____   is
vain. _____   And   the   sun - shine   we've   been   wait - ing   for _____   will

Additional Lyrics

3. But I'm frightened for your children.
   And the life that we are living is in vain.
   And the sunshine we've been waiting for will turn to rain.
   Where the final line is over and it's certain the curtain's gonna fall,
   I can hide inside your sweet, sweet love forevermore.

Rikki Don't Lose That Number

Words and Music by Walter Becker and Donald Fagen

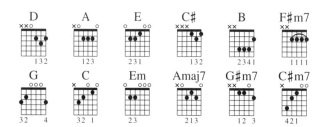

Strum Pattern: 3
Pick Pattern: 3

Intro
Moderately

Verse

1. We hear you're leav-ing, that's O. K.
2. *See Additional Lyrics*

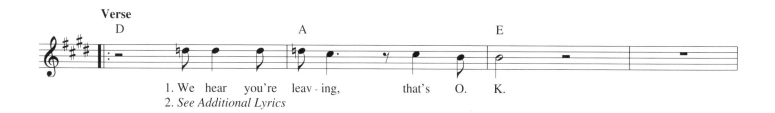

I thought our lit-tle wild time had just be-gun.

I guess you kind of scared your-self, you turn ___ and run. ___

But if you have a change of heart... ___

Chorus

Rik-ki, don't lose that num-ber; you don't wan-na call no-bod-y else. ___

Send it off in a let - ter to your - self.

Rik - ki, don't lose that num - ber; it's the on - ly one you own. __ You might

use it if you feel bet - ter when you get _____ home.

To Coda ⊕   **Bridge**
You tell your-self you're not my kind, _____

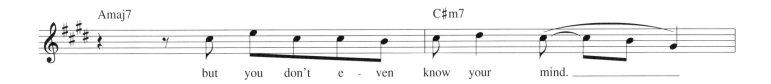
but you don't e - ven know your mind. _____

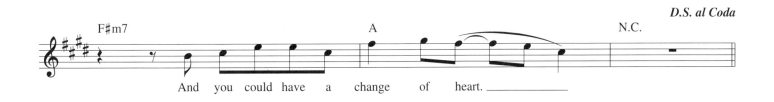
D.S. al Coda
And you could have a change of heart. _____

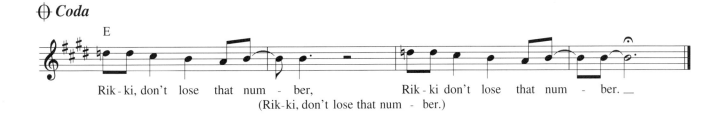
⊕ *Coda*
Rik - ki, don't lose that num - ber,   Rik - ki don't lose that num - ber. __
(Rik - ki, don't lose that num - ber.)

Additional Lyrics

2. I have a friend in town, he's heard your name.
We can go out driving on Slow Hand Row.
We could stay inside and play games, I don't know.
And you could have a change of heart.

Should I Stay or Should I Go

Words and Music by Joe Strummer and Mick Jones

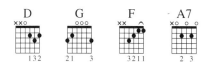

Strum Pattern: 6
Pick Pattern: 5

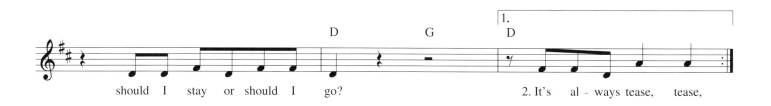

And if I stay, it will be dou - ble. So you've got to let me

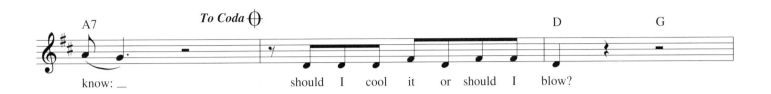

To Coda

know: __ should I cool it or should I blow?

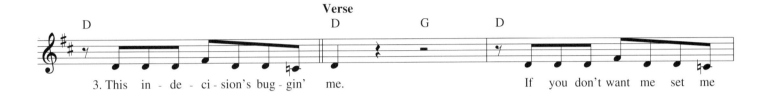

Verse

3. This in - de - ci - sion's bug - gin' me. If you don't want me set me

free. Ex - act - ly who'm I s'posed to be? ____

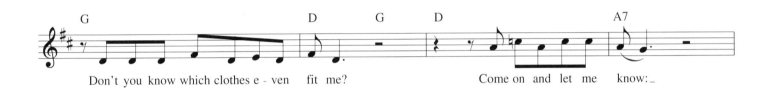

Don't you know which clothes e - ven fit me? Come on and let me know: _

D.S. al Coda

should I cool it or should I blow? Should I stay or should I

Coda

should I stay or should I go?

Additional Lyrics

2. It's always tease, tease, tease.
   You're happy when I'm on my knees.
   One day is fine and next is black.
   So if you want me off your back,
   Well, come on and let me know:
   Should I stay or should I go?

Space Oddity

Words and Music by David Bowie

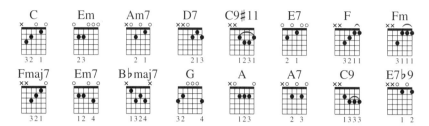

Strum Pattern: 5
Pick Pattern: 1

Intro
Moderately Slow

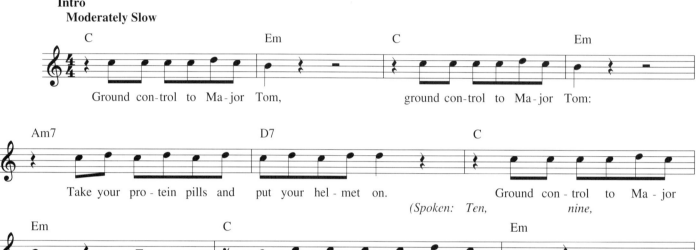

Ground con-trol to Ma-jor Tom,   ground con-trol to Ma-jor Tom:

Take your pro-tein pills and put your hel-met on.   Ground con-trol to Ma-jor
(Spoken: Ten,   nine,

Tom: Com-men-cing count down: En-gines on.
eight,   seven,   six,   five,   four,   three,

Check ig-ni-tion and may God's love be with you.
two,   one.   Lift   off!)

Verse

1. This is ground con-trol to Ma-jor Tom;   you've real-ly made the
2. *See Additional Lyrics*

grade! _____   And the pa-pers want to know whose shirts you wear. _   Now it's

time to leave the cap-sule if you dare. _____   day. _____   For

Additional Lyrics

2. This is Major Tom to ground control;
I'm stepping through the door.
And I'm floating in a most peculiar way.
And the stars look very different today.

Start Me Up

Words and Music by Mick Jagger and Keith Richards

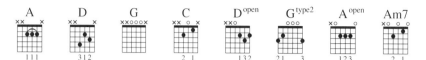

Strum Pattern: 3
Pick Pattern: 3

Intro
Moderately

If you start me up,

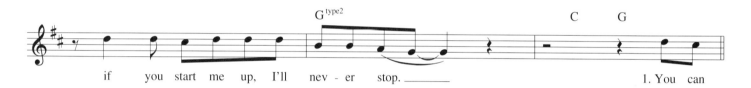

if you start me up, I'll nev-er stop. _____ 1. You can

Verse

start me up, _____ you can start me up I'll nev-er stop. _____
2. *See Additional Lyrics*

I've been run-ning hot, _____ you got me just a-bout to
3. *See Additional Lyrics*

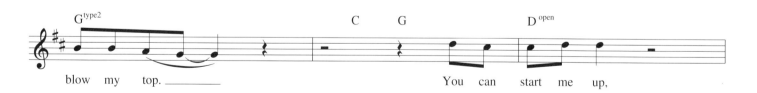

blow my top. _____ You can start me up,

you can start me up, I nev-er stop, nev-er stop, nev-er stop, nev-er stop. __

You make a grown _ man cry, _____ you make a grown _ man

cry, _____ you make a grown _ man cry, _____ spread out the oil,

the gas - o - line. I want a smooth ride in a mean, mean ma - chine. _____

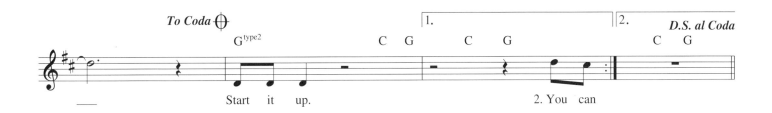

_____ Start it up. 2. You can

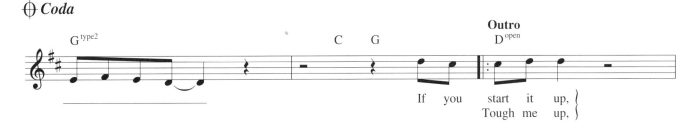

If you start it up, ⎱
Tough me up, ⎰

love the day when we will nev - er stop, nev - er stop, nev - er, nev - er, nev - er stop.

Additional Lyrics

2. You can start me up, kick on the starter, give it all you've got.
I can't compete with the riders in the other heats.
You rough it up, if you like it you can slide it up, slide it up, slide it up.
Don't make a grown man cry, don't make a grown man cry,
Don't make a grown man cry, my eyes dilate my lips so green,
My hands are greasy, she's a mean, mean machine. Start it up.

3. Start me up, ah, you've got to, you've got to, never, never, never stop.
Start it up, ah, start it up, never, never, never.
You make a grown man cry, you make a grown man cry,
You make a grown man cry, ride like the wind at double speed,
I'll take you places that you've never, never seen.

Strutter

Words and Music by Paul Stanley and Gene Simmons

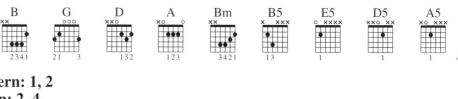

Strum Pattern: 1, 2
Pick Pattern: 2, 4

Intro
Moderate Rock

1., 3. I know a thing or two a - bout her.
2. See Additional Lyrics

I know she'll on - ly make you cry.

She'll let you walk the street be - side her. Ooh. But when she

walks she'll pass you by. Ev - 'ry - bod - y says she's look - in' good,

and the la - dy knows it's un - der - stood. Strut - ter.

Additional Lyrics

2. She wears her satins like a lady.
   She gets her way like a child.
   You take her home and she says, "Maybe, baby."
   She takes you down and drives you wild.

Sultans of Swing

Words and Music by Mark Knopfler

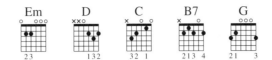

Strum Pattern: 1
Pick Pattern: 2

Intro
Bright Rock

1. You get a

shiv - er in the dark, it's a - rain - in' in the park, but mean - time,

2., 3., 4., 5., 7. *See Additional Lyrics*
6., 8. *Instrumental*

south of the riv - er you stop and you hold ev - 'ry - thing. __

A band is blow - in' Dix - ie dou - ble four __ time.

You feel all right when you hear that mu - sic ring. __

|1., 3.

2. Well, now you   Way on down __ south,

way on down south Lon - don town. __

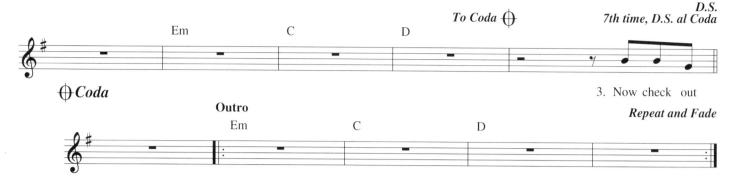

To Coda ⊕

D.S.
7th time, D.S. al Coda

| Em | C | D |

⊕ *Coda*

Outro

| Em | C | D |

3. Now check out

Repeat and Fade

Additional Lyrics

2. Well, now you step inside but you don't see too many faces.
Comin' in out of the rain you hear the jazz go down.
Competition, in other places,
Uh, but the horns, they blowin' that sound.
Way on down south, way on down south, London town.

3. Now check out Guitar George, he knows all the chords.
But he's strictly rhythm, he doesn't want to make it cry or sing.
They say and old guitar is all he can afford,
When he gets up under the lights, to play his thing.

4. And Harry doesn't mind if he doesn't make the scene.
He's got a daytime job, he's doin' all right.
He can play the honky-tonk like anything,
Savin' it up for Friday night
With the Sultans, with the Sultans of swing.

5. Then a crowd of young boys, they're foolin' around in the corner,
Drunk and dressed in their best brown baggies and their platform soles.
They don't give a damn about any trumpet playin' band.
It ain't what they call Rock and Roll.
And the Sultans, yeah the Sultans play creole. Creole.

7. And then the man steps right up to the microphone
And says at last just as the time bell rings.
"Good-night, now it's time to go home."
Then he makes it fast with one more thing.
"We are the Sultans, we are the Sultans of Swing."

Sweet Emotion

Words and Music by Steven Tyler and Tom Hamilton

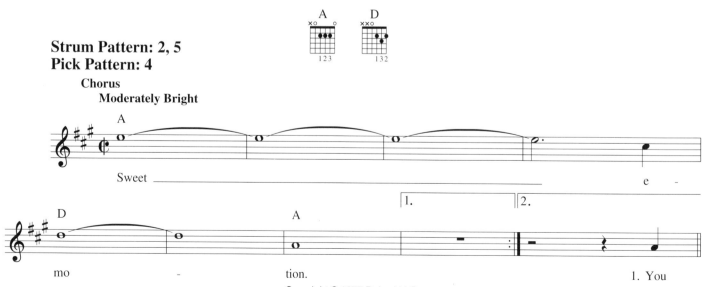

Strum Pattern: 2, 5
Pick Pattern: 4

Chorus
Moderately Bright

Sweet _____ e -

mo - tion.

1. You

Additional Lyrics

2. Some sweet talkin' mama with a face like a gent
   Said my get up and go must have got up and went.
   Well, I got good news, she's a real good liar,
   'Cause my backstage boogie set yo' pants on fire.

3. I pulled into town in a police car;
   Your daddy said I took you just a little too far.
   You're tellin' her things but your girlfriend lied;
   You can't catch me 'cause the rabbit done died.

4. Stand in front just a shakin' your ass;
   I'll take you backstage, you can drink from my glass.
   I'm talkin' 'bout somethin' you can sure understand,
   'Cause a month on the road and I'll be eatin' from your hand.

Susie-Q

Words and Music by Dale Hawkins, Stan Lewis and Eleanor Broadwater

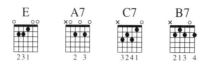

Strum Pattern: 3
Pick Pattern: 3

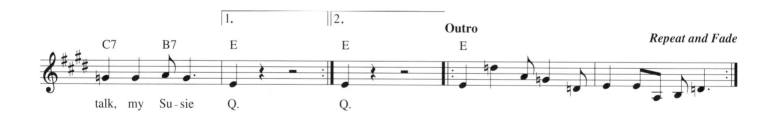

Additional Lyrics

2. Well, say that you'll be true.
   Well, say that you'll be true.
   Well, say that you'll be true.
   And never leave me blue,
   My Susie Q.

Ticket to Ride

Words and Music by John Lennon and Paul McCartney

Strum Pattern: 4
Pick Pattern: 1

Additional Lyrics

2., 4. She said that livin' with me is bringin' her down, yeah.
For she would never be free when I was around.

Time

Words and Music by Roger Waters, Nicholas Mason, David Gilmour and Rick Wright

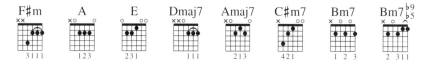

Strum Pattern: 6
Pick Pattern: 5

Verse
Moderately

1. Tick-ing a - way ___ the mo-ments that make up a dull ___ day;
2. *See Additional Lyrics*

frit - ter and waste ___ the hours ___ in an off-hand way. ___

Kick-ing a - round ___ on a piece of ground ___ in your home town;

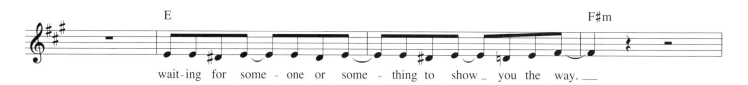

wait-ing for some - one or some - thing to show ___ you the way. ___

Chorus
Half-Time Feel

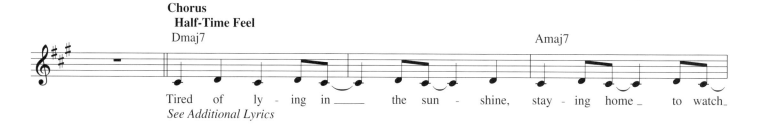

Tired of ly - ing in ___ the sun - shine, stay-ing home ___ to watch ___
See Additional Lyrics

___ the rain, you are young and life ___ is long, and there is time to kill ___

___ to - day. And then one day, you find ___ ten years have got

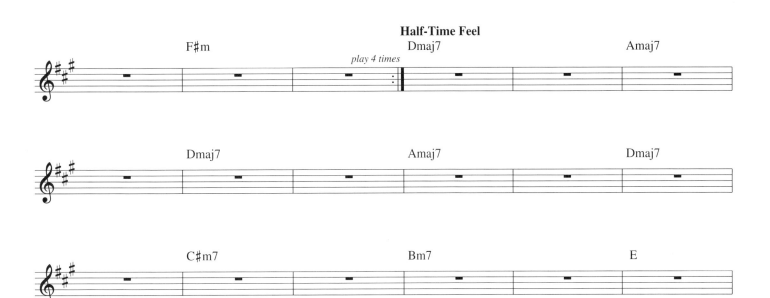

Additional Lyrics

2. And you run and you run to catch up with the sun, but it's sinking;
   Racing around to come up behind you again.
   The sun is the same in a relative way, but you're older.
   Shorter of breath and one day closer to death.

Chorus Ev'ry year is getting shorter, never seem to find the time.
   Plans that either come to naught or half a page of scribbled lines.
   Hanging on in quiet desperation is the English way.
   The time is gone. The song is over.
   Thought I'd something more to say.

(So) Tired of Waiting for You

Words and Music by Ray Davies

Strum Pattern: 3
Pick Pattern: 3

Turn! Turn! Turn!
(To Everything There Is a Season)

Words from the Book of Ecclesiastes
Adaptation and Music by Pete Seeger

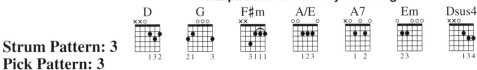

Strum Pattern: 3
Pick Pattern: 3

Intro
Moderately

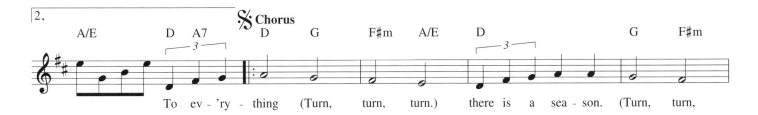

To ev - 'ry - thing (Turn, turn, turn.) there is a sea - son. (Turn, turn,

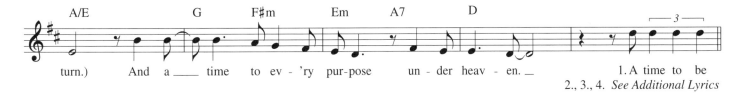

turn.) And a _____ time to ev - 'ry pur - pose un - der heav - en. _____   1. A time to be
                                                                              2., 3., 4. *See Additional Lyrics*

Verse

born, a time _ to die;   a time to plant, a time _ to reap;   a time to

kill, a time _ to heal;   a time to laugh, _____ a time _____ to

weep. _____   To ev - 'ry -

Additional Lyrics

2. A time to build up, a time to break down;
   A time to dance, a time to mourn;
   A time to cast away stones;
   A time to gather stones together.

3. A time of love, a time of hate.
   A time of war, a time of peace.
   A time you may embrace,
   A time to refrain from embracing.

4. A time to gain, a time to lose.
   A time to mend, a time to sew.
   A time for love, a time for hate.
   A time for peace; I swear it's not too late.

Wake Up Little Susie

Words and Music by Boudleaux Bryant and Felice Bryant

Wake up, lit - tle Su - sie. —

Additional Lyrics

3. The movie wasn't so hot.
It didn't have much of a plot.
We fell asleep, our goose is cooked,
Our reputation is shot.
Wake up, little Susie.
Wake up, little Susie.

Walk Away

Words and Music by Joe Walsh

Strum Pattern: 3, 5
Pick Pattern: 3, 5

Verse
Moderate Rock

1. Tak-in' my time, ___ choos-in' my line, ___ try'n' to de-cide ___ what to do. ___
2., 3. *See Additional Lyrics*

Looks like my style, ___ don't wan-na get off, ___

got my-self hung ___ up on you. ___ 1., 3. Seems to me ___ you don't
2. *See Additional Lyrics*

wan-na talk a-bout ___ it. Seems to me ___ you just turn your pret-ty head ___ and walk a-

To Coda

way. ___

Chorus

Seems to me ___ you don't wan-na talk a-bout ___ it. Seems to

me ___ you just turn your pret-ty head ___ and walk a-way. ___

D.C. al Coda

3. I got to

MCA Music Publishing

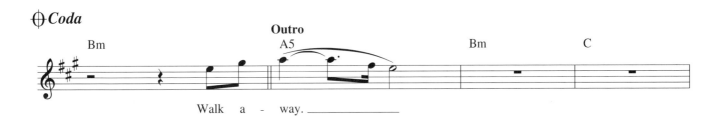

Additional Lyrics

2. Places I've known, things that I'm growin',
   Don't taste the same without you.
   I got myself in the worst mess I been in,
   And I find myself startin' to doubt you.

Chorus 2. Seems to me don't go mad here come the mornin'.
   Seems to me you just forget what was said and greet the day.

3. I got to cool myself down, stompin' around.
   Thinkin' some words, I can't blame ya.
   Meet ya halfway, I got nothin' to say,
   Still I don't s'pose I can blame ya.

Wanted Dead or Alive

Words and Music by Jon Bon Jovi and Richie Sambora

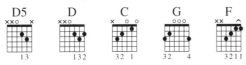

Strum Pattern: 1, 3
Pick Pattern: 2, 4

 Verse
Moderately

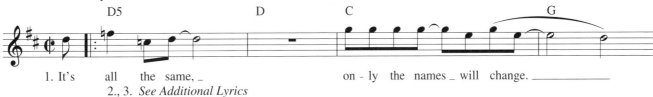

1. It's all the same, _ on - ly the names _ will change. _____
2., 3. *See Additional Lyrics*

Ev - 'ry day ___ it seems we're wast - ing a - way. An -

Additional Lyrics

2. Sometimes I sleep,
   Sometimes it's not for days.
   The people I meet always go their sep'rate ways.
   Sometimes, you tell the day by the bottle that you drink.
   And times when you're alone, all you do is think.

3. And I walk these streets,
   A loaded six string on my back.
   I've seen a million faces, and I've rocked them all.
   I've been ev'rywhere, still I'm standing tall.
   I play for keeps, 'cause I might not make it back.

Young Americans

Words and Music by David Bowie

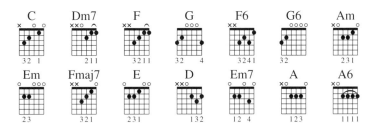

Strum Pattern: 3
Pick Pattern: 3

Intro
Heavy Beat

Verse

1. They pulled in just be-hind the fridge, _ he lays her down. _ He frowns, _

"Gee, my life's a fun - ny thing. Am I _____ still too young?"

He kissed her then and there; _ she took his ring, _ took his ba - bies. It

took him min - utes, took her no - where. _ Heav - en knows, _ she'd have tak -

Chorus

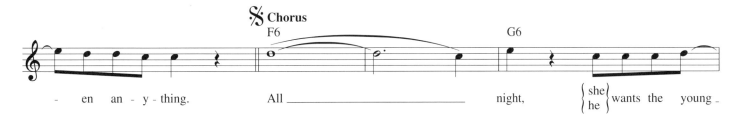

- en an - y - thing. All _____ night, { she } { he } wants the young _

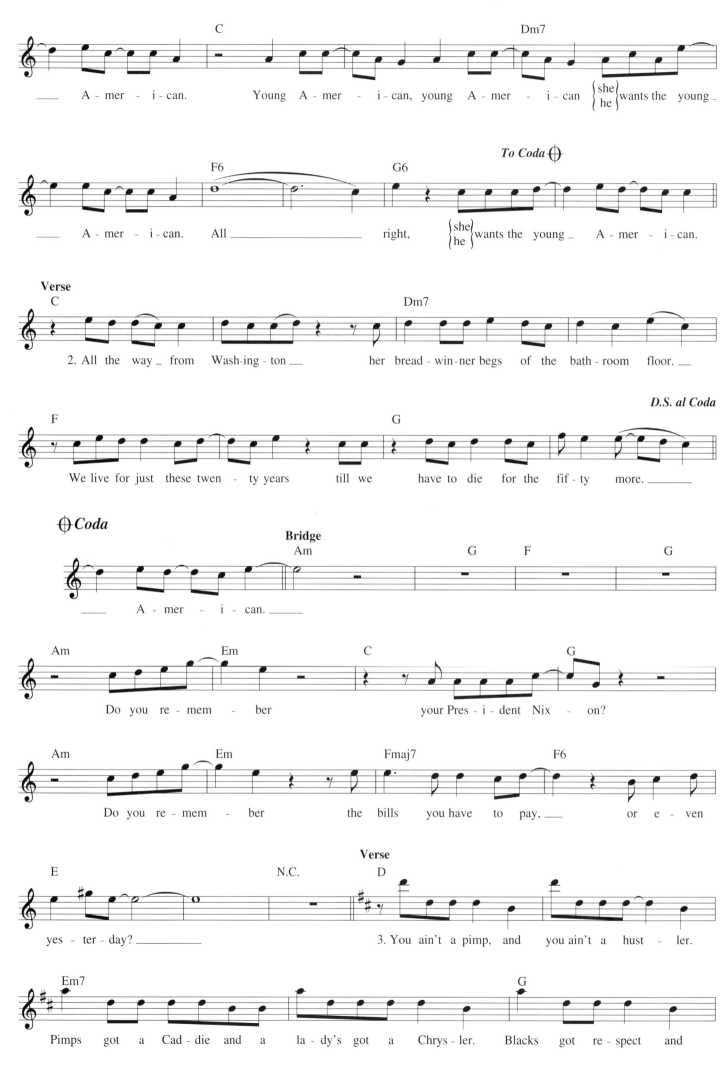

American. Young A-mer-i-can, young A-mer-i-can {she/he} wants the young

American. All _____ right, {she/he} wants the young ___ A-mer-i-can.

Verse

2. All the way ___ from Wash-ing - ton ___ her bread-win-ner begs of the bath-room floor. ___

D.S. al Coda

We live for just these twen - ty years till we have to die for the fif - ty more. _____

Coda

Bridge

___ A - mer - i - can. ___

Do you re - mem - ber your Pres - i - dent Nix - on?

Do you re - mem - ber the bills you have to pay, ___ or e - ven

Verse

yes - ter - day? _____ 3. You ain't a pimp, and you ain't a hust - ler.

Pimps got a Cad - die and a la - dy's got a Chrys - ler. Blacks got re - spect and

We Gotta Get Out of This Place

Words and Music by Barry Mann and Cynthia Weil

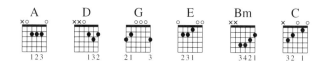

Strum Pattern: 6
Pick Pattern: 4

Verse
Moderately

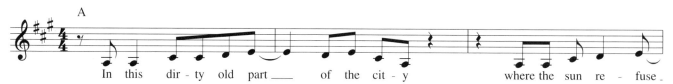

In this dir-ty old part ___ of the cit-y where the sun re-fuse

___ to shine, ___ peo-ple tell me there ain't ___ no use ___ in tryin'. ___

___ My lit-tle girl, ___ you're so young and ___ pret-ty.

And one thing I know ___ is true: ___ you'll be dead be-fore ___

___ your time is through. ___ See my dad-dy in bed. ___

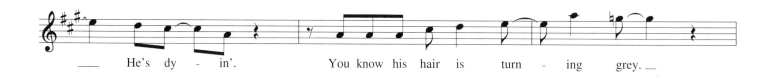

___ He's dy-in'. You know his hair is turn-ing grey. ___

He's been work - ing and slav - ing his life a - way. ____

Pre-Chorus

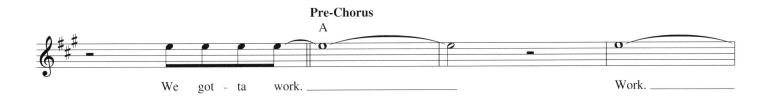

We got - ta work. _____ Work. _____

____ We got - ta work. _____ Work, work,

Chorus

work, work. We got - ta get out ____ of this place ___

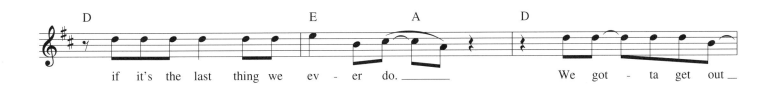

if it's the last thing we ev - er do. _____ We got - ta get out ___

___ of this place. ___ Girl, there's a bet - ter life for me and you. ___

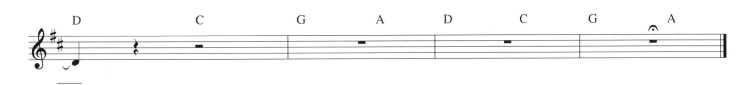

What I Like About You

Words and Music by Michael Skill, Wally Palamarchuk and James Marinos

154

Additional Lyrics

3. What I like about you,
   You keep me warm at night.
   Never wanna let you go,
   Know you make me feel alright. Yeah!

What's Your Name

Words and Music by Gary Rossington and Ronnie Van Zant

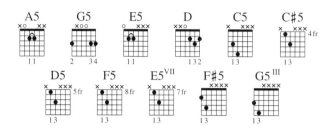

Strum Pattern: 1, 6
Pick Pattern: 4, 5

Verse

Moderate Rock

1. Well, it's eight o' clock in ___ Boi - se, I - da - ho. ___
2., 3. *See Additional Lyrics*

I found my li - mo driv - er, "Mis - ter, take us to the show." ___

___ I done ___ made some plans ___ for la - ter on ___ to - night. ___

___ I'll find a lit - tle queen ___ and I ___

___ know I can treat her right. ___

What's your name, ___
What's your name, ___
What was your name, ___

Chorus

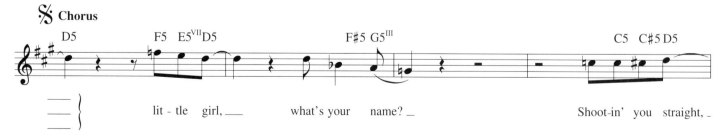

___ lit - tle girl, ___ what's your name? ___ Shoot - in' you straight, ___

MCA Music Publishing

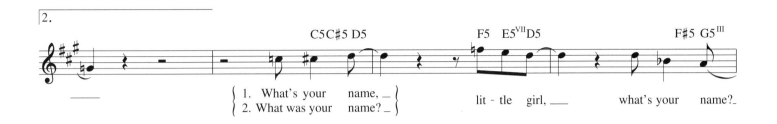

lit - tle girl, — { 1., 3. won't 'cha do the same? __
{ 2., 4. well, there ain't no shame. _

{ 1. What's your name, _ }
{ 2. What was your name? _ } lit - tle girl, ___ what's your name?_

Shoot - in' you straight, _ lit - tle girl, _

___ won't 'cha do the same?___ What's your name, _

⊕ Coda

___ won't 'cha do the same?___ Whew!

Additional Lyrics

2. Back at the hotel, Lord we got such a mess.
   It seems that one of the crew had a go with one of the guests, ah yes.
   Well, the police said we can't drink in the bar, what a shame.
   Won't 'cha come upstairs, girl, and have a drink of champagne?

3. Nine o'clock and the next day I'm ready to go.
   I got six hundred miles to ride to do one more show, oh no.
   Can I get you a taxi home? It sure was grand.
   When I come back here next year I wanna see you again.

White Room

Words and Music by Jack Bruce and Pete Brown

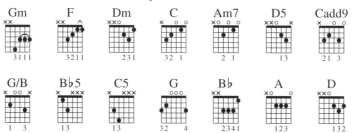

Strum Pattern: 3
Pick Pattern: 3

Intro
Moderately

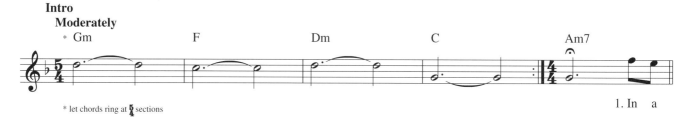

* let chords ring at 5/4 sections

1. In a

white room   with black cur-tains   near the sta - tion.   Black roof coun - try,   no gold
2., 3. *See Additional Lyrics*

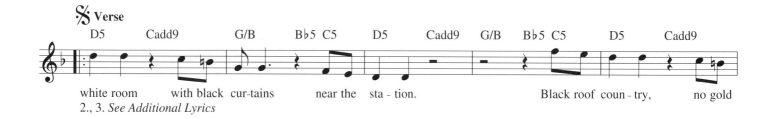

pave-ments,   tired _ star-lings.   Sil-ver hor - ses   ran down moon-beams   in your

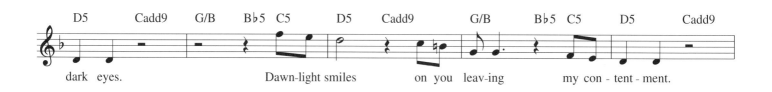

dark eyes.   Dawn-light smiles   on you leav-ing   my con - tent - ment.

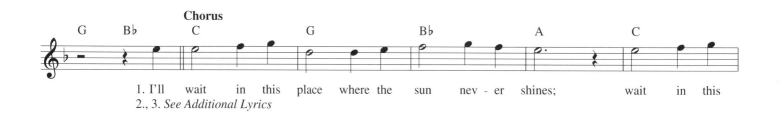

1. I'll wait in this place where the sun nev - er shines;   wait in this
2., 3. *See Additional Lyrics*

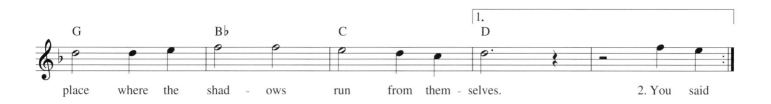

place   where   the   shad - ows   run   from   them - selves.   2. You   said

selves.

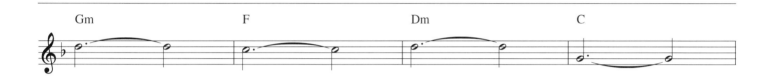

3.   At   the   selves.

Additional Lyrics

2. You said no strings could secure you at the station.
   Platform ticket, restless diesels, goodbye windows.
   I walked into such a sad time at the station.
   As I walked out, felt my own need just beginning.

Chorus 2. I'll wait in the queue when the trains come back,
   Lie with you where the shadows run from themselves.

3. At the party, she was kindness in the hard crowd.
   Consolation for the old wound now forgotten.
   Yellow tigers crouched in jungles in the dark eyes.
   She's just dressing, goodbye windows, tired starlings.

Chorus 3. I'll sleep in this place with the lonely crowd.
   Lie in the dark where the shadows run from themselves.

Wonderful Tonight

Words and Music by Eric Clapton

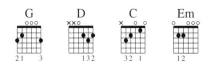

Strum Pattern: 4
Pick Pattern: 1

Intro
Moderately

Verse

1. It's late in the eve - ning; she's won-d'ring what clothes _
2., 3. *See Additional Lyrics*

_ to wear. _ She puts on her make - up and brush-es her long _

_ blonde hair. _ And then she asks _ me, "Do I look all right?" _

To Coda

_ And I say, "Yes, you look won - der - ful _ to - night." _

1.

Additional Lyrics

2. We go to a party, and ev'ryone turns to see.
   This beautiful lady is walking around with me.
   And then she asks me, "Do you feel alright?"
   And I say, "Yes, I feel wonderful tonight."

3. It's time to go home now, and I've got an aching head.
   So I give her the car keys, and she helps me to bed.
   And then I tell her, as I turn out the light,
   I say, "My darling, you are wonderful tonight."
   Oh, my darling, you are wonderful tonight.

You Give Love a Bad Name

Words and Music by Jon Bon Jovi, Richie Sambora and Desmond Child

Strum Pattern: 4
Pick Pattern: 3

Intro
Moderate Rock

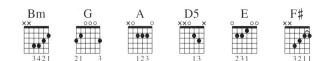

Shot through the heart ___ and you're to ___ blame. Dar-lin', you give love ___ a

bad name.

Verse

1. An an-gel's smile ___ is what you sell. You
2. *See Additional Lyrics*

prom-ise me heav-en, then put me through hell. Chains of ___ love ___ got a

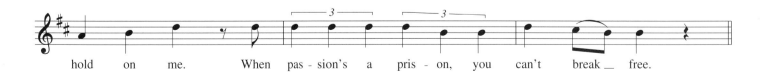

hold on me. When pas-sion's a pris-on, you can't break ___ free.

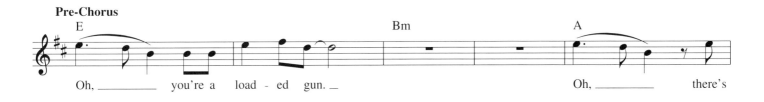

Pre-Chorus

Oh, _____ you're a load- ed gun. _____ Oh, _____ there's

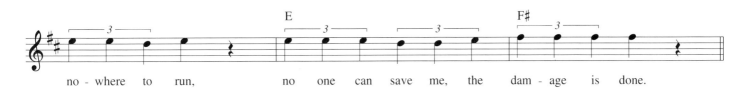

no - where to run, no one can save me, the dam- age is done.

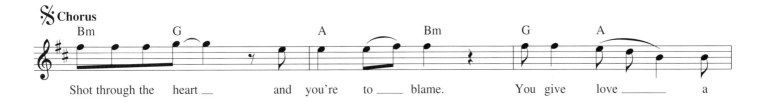

Chorus

Shot through the heart ___ and you're to ___ blame. You give love _____ a

To Coda

bad name. (Bad name.) I play my part ___ and you play your _ game. You give love _____ a

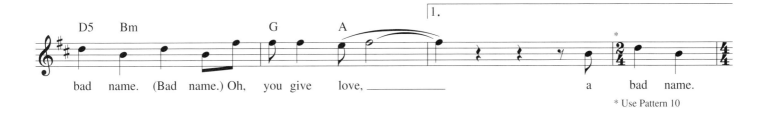

1.

bad name. (Bad name.) Oh, you give love, _____ a bad name.

* Use Pattern 10

2.

D.S. al Coda

2. You ___

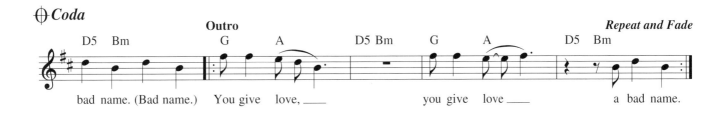

Coda

Outro

Repeat and Fade

bad name. (Bad name.) You give love, ___ you give love ___ a bad name.

Additional Lyrics

2. You paint your smile on your lips.
Blood-red nails on your fingertips.
A schoolboy's dream, you act so shy.
Your very first kiss was your first kiss goodbye.

You're My Best Friend

Words and Music by John Deacon

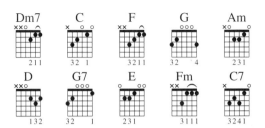

Strum Pattern: 3
Pick Pattern: 3

Intro
Moderately

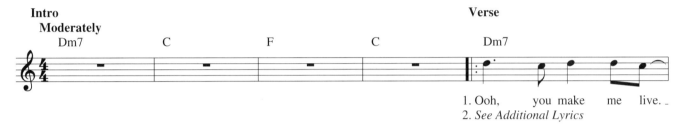

1. Ooh, you make me live.
2. *See Additional Lyrics*

What - ev - er this world can give to me. __ It's you, you're all I __ see. __

Ooh, you make me live __ now, hon - ey. Ooh, you make me live. __

Ooh, __ you're the best __ friend __ that I __ ev - er had. __ I've

been with you such a long time. __ You're my sun - shine __ and I want __

__ you to know __ that my feel - ings are true. __ I real - ly love you.

* Use Pattern 10

Oh, _____ you're my best _____ friend. _____ Ooh, you make me live. _

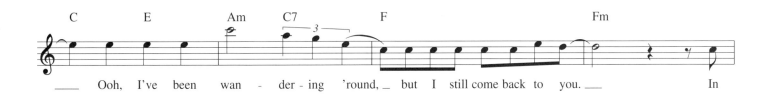

_____ Ooh, I've been wan - der - ing 'round, _ but I still come back to you. _____ In

rain or shine _____ you've stood by me, girl, _ I'm hap - py at home, _ you're my best _

_____ friend. _ Ooh, ooh, _ you're my best _

_____ friend. _ Ooh, you make me live. _____ Ooh, you're my best friend. _

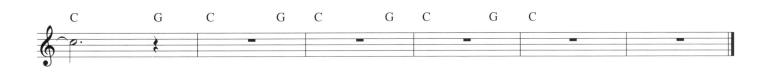

Additional Lyrics

2. Ooh, you make me live.
   Whenever this world is cruel to me.
   I got you to help me forgive.
   Ooh, you make me live now, honey.
   Ooh, you make me live.
   Ooh, you're the first one when things turn out bad.
   You know I'll never be lonely, you're my only one.
   And I love the things, I really love the things that you do.
   Oh, you're my best friend.

THE GUITAR TECHNIQUES SERIES

The series designed to get you started! Each book clearly presents essential concepts, highlighting specific elements of guitar playing and music theory. Most books include tablature and standard notation.

Acoustic Rock For Guitar

The acoustic guitar has found renewed popularity in contemporary rock. From ballads to metal, you'll find many artists adding that distinctive acoustic sound to their songs. This book demonstrates the elements of good acoustic guitar playing – both pick and fingerstyle – that are used in rock today. Topics include Chords and Variations, Strumming Styles, Picking Patterns, Scales and Runs, and much more.
00699327.....................................$6.95

Arpeggios For Guitar

An introduction to the basics, including: Performance etudes; one-octave arpeggios; five-and six-string forms; string-skipping forms; and more.
00695044 ....$6.95

Basic Blues For Guitar

This book taps into the history of great blues guitarists like B.B. King and Muddy Waters. It teaches the guitarist blues accompaniments, bar chords and how to improvise leads.
00699008 ....$6.95

Music Theory For Guitar

Music theory is the cornerstone in understanding music. But how does a guitar player relate it to the guitar? This volume answers that question. Concepts of scale, harmony, chords, intervals and modes are presented in the context of applying them to the guitar. This book will open the door to not only understanding the fundamentals of music, but also the world of playing the guitar with more insight and intelligence.
00699329.....................................$7.95

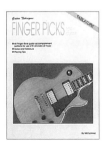

Finger Picks For Guitar

A convenient reference to 47 fingerstyle guitar accompaniment patterns for use with all types of music. In standard notation and tablature. Also includes playing tips.
00699125 ....$6.95

Lead Blues Licks

This book examines a number of blues licks in the styles of such greats as B.B. King, Albert King, Stevie Ray Vaughan, Eric Clapton, Chuck Berry, and more. Varying these licks and combining them with others can improve lead playing and can be used in rock styles as well as blues. Clearly written in notes and tab, you'll progress from the standard blues progression and blues scale to the various techniques of bending, fast pull offs and hammer-ons, double stops, and more.
00699325.....................................$6.95

Lead Rock Licks For Guitar

Learn the latest hot licks played by great guitarists, including Jeff Beck, Neal Schon (of Journey), Andy Summers (Police), and Randy Rhoads (Ozzy Osbourne). The guitarist can use each lick in this book as building material to further create new and more exciting licks of their own.
00699007 ....$6.95

Rhythms For Blues For Guitar

This book brings to life everything you need to play blues rhythm patterns, in a quick, handy and easy-to-use book. Everything from basic blues progressions to turnarounds, including swing, shuffle, straight eighths rhythms, plus small, altered and sliding chord patterns. All are presented in the style of many of the great blues and rock blues legends. Includes notes and tab.
00699326.....................................$6.95

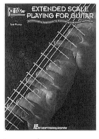

Extended Scale Playing For Guitar

An innovative approach to expanding left hand technique by Joe Puma. The sliding first finger technique presented in this book will give players a new and broader outlook on the guitar. The book explores a variety of scales – major, minor, half-tone/whole-tone – and more.
00697237.....................................$7.95

Right Hand Techniques

Through basic alternate, sweep and cross picking patterns, 10 chord arpeggios, palm muting and fingerstyle techniques, this book presents everything you need to know in getting started with the basic techniques needed to play every type of music. Additional topics include rhythm, rake and fingerstyle techniques. A real power packed technique book!
00699328.....................................$6.95

Rock Chords For Guitar

Learn to play open-string, heavy metal power chords and bar chords with this book. This book introduces most of the chords needed to play today's rock 'n' roll. There are very clear fingering diagrams and chord frames on the top of each page. Empty staves at the bottom of each page allow the player to draw in his own chord patterns.
00689649 ....$6.95

Rock Scales For Guitar

This book contains all of the Rock, Blues, and Country scales employed in today's music. It shows the guitarist how scales are constructed and designed, how scales connect and relate to one another, how and where to use the scales they are learning, all of the possible scale forms for each different scale type, how to move each scale to new tonal areas and much, much more.
00699164 ....$6.95

Strums For Guitar

A handy guide that features 48 guitar strumming patterns for use with all styles of music. Also includes playing tips.
00699135 ....$6.95

FOR MORE INFORMATION, SEE YOUR LOCAL MUSIC DEALER, OR WRITE TO:

HAL•LEONARD® CORPORATION
7777 W. BLUEMOUND RD. P.O. BOX 13819 MILWAUKEE, WI 53213

Prices, book contents & availability subject to change without notice.

0796

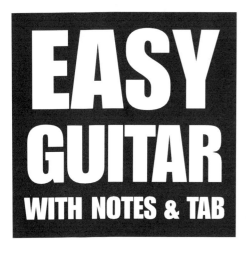

EASY GUITAR
WITH NOTES & TAB

This series features simplified arrangements with notes, TAB, chord charts, and strum and pick patterns.

00702026	90s Rock For Easy Guitar	$12.95
00702002	Acoustic Rock Hits	$12.95
00702001	Best of Aerosmith	$12.95
00702040	Best of Allman Brothers	$8.95
00702043	Best of Johnny Cash	$8.95
00702033	Best Of Steven Curtis Chapman	$12.95
00702028	Christmas Classics	$7.95
00702090	Eric Clapton's Best	$9.95
00702086	Eric Clapton – Live Acoustic	$10.95
00702048	Christmas Cheer	$10.95
00702016	Classic Blues For Easy Guitar	$12.95
00702053	Best of Patsy Cline	$8.95
00702006	Contemporary Christian Favorites	$9.95
00702091	Contemporary Country Ballads	$9.95
00702089	Contemporary Country Pickin'	$9.95
00702065	Contemporary Women of Country	$9.95
00702084	Best Of Def Leppard	$12.95
00702085	Disney Movie Hits	$9.95
00702041	Favorite Hymns	$9.95
00702057	Golden Age of Rock	$8.95
00699374	Gospel Favorites	$14.95
00702050	Great Classical Themes	$6.95
00702066	Great Hits of 1996-1997	$8.95
00699394	Guitar Wedding Collection	$14.95
00702037	Hits of the '50s	$10.95
00702035	Hits of the '60s	$10.95
00702046	Hits of the '70s	$10.95
00702047	Hits of the '80s	$8.95
00702054	Best of Hootie and the Blowfish	$9.95

00702059	Disney's The Hunchback of Notre Dame	$10.95
00702032	International Songs	$12.95
00702045	Jailhouse Rock, Kansas City and Other Hits by Leiber & Stoller	$8.95
00702021	Jazz Standards	$14.95
00702051	Jock Rock	$8.95
00702087	New Best Of Billy Joel	$9.95
00702088	New Best Of Elton John	$9.95
00702011	Best Of Carole King	$12.95
00702003	Kiss For Easy Guitar	$9.95
00699003	Lion King & Pocahontas	$9.95
00702005	Best Of Andrew Lloyd Webber	$10.95
00702061	Love Songs of the 50s & 60s	$8.95
00702062	Love Songs of the 70s & 80s	$8.95
00702063	Love Songs of the 90s	$9.95
00702052	Alanis Morissette – Jagged Little Pill	$10.95
00702039	Movie Themes	$10.95
00702067	The Nutcracker Suite	$5.95
00702030	Best Of Roy Orbison	$12.95
00702004	Rockin' Elvis	$9.95
00699415	Best Of Queen	$12.95
00702093	Rolling Stones Collection	$17.95
00702092	Best Of The Rolling Stones	$9.95
00702010	Best Of Rod Stewart	$12.95
00702049	Best Of George Strait	$10.95
00702042	Today's Christian Favorites	$8.95
00702029	Top Hits Of '95-'96 For Easy Guitar	$12.95
00702034	Top Hits Of '96-'97 For Easy Guitar	$12.95
00702007	TV Tunes For Guitar	$12.95

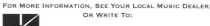

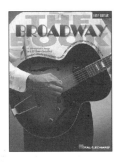

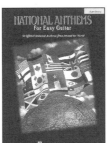